CASHED UP! with

COMMERCIAL PROPERTY

A STEP-BY-STEP GUIDE TO BUILDING A
CASH FLOW POSITIVE PORTFOLIO

HELEN TARRANT

First published in 2023 by John Wiley & Sons Australia, Ltd
Level 1, 155 Cremorne St, Richmond Vic 3121

Typeset in Kepler Std 12/16pt

© John Wiley & Sons Australia, Ltd 2023

The moral rights of the author have been asserted

ISBN: 978-1-119-91034-3

A catalogue record for this book is available from the National Library of Australia

Cover design by Wiley
Cover image by ROJO Design Architects

Disclaimer
The material in this publication is of the nature of general comment only, and does not represent professional advice. It is not intended to provide specific guidance for particular circumstances and it should not be relied on as the basis for any decision to take action or not take action on any matter which it covers. Readers should obtain professional advice where appropriate, before making any such decision. To the maximum extent permitted by law, the author and publisher disclaim all responsibility and liability to any person, arising directly or indirectly from any person taking or not taking action based on the information in this publication.

CONTENTS

Special thanks   *v*

Introduction   *vii*

1   My path to commercial property   1

2   Why commercial property?   21

3   Commercial property vs residential property   35

4   Commercial property strategies   55

5   Cash flow is the foundation   67

6   Would you like some growth with that?   87

7   Types of commercial property   103

8   Finance and structure   117

9   Investing through your SMSF   133

10   Putting the deal together   159

11   Others just like you   183

12   Uplift projects   219

13   Sailing off into the sunset   231

Conclusion: If they can do it, so can you…   *241*

Now it's your turn!   *245*

Resources   *251*

Index   *253*

SPECIAL THANKS

I would like to say a special thank you to everyone at Wiley who has been behind the scenes helping me put this book together. I am a new author and without your help this wouldn't have happened.

Further, I want to say a special thank you to the following people who have helped to make my business and my life successful.

John Tarrant — without you I wouldn't have started. I will always be grateful.

Stephen Johnson — without you, your help and constant presence since we met, I wouldn't have gone to the next level. Together we will make Unikorn Commercial Property great — I owe you a debt of gratitude forever.

Wilma Dancel — you are like family and my right-hand lady. My business wouldn't work without you. You make my life easier and help me to achieve the big goals by taking care of the little things in the business.

My team — everyone in the office and offshore — without you, Unikorn Commercial Property wouldn't run. You make our clients happy and loved and most of all you help to implement my strategies and vision.

My parents — Mum and Dad, it is because of you that I want to help everyday Australians retire early and enjoy their retirement. My childhood was magical — I learnt so much growing up differently to everyone else. I wouldn't be me today without the two of you.

Max and Jett — you are the reason I am building Unikorn Commercial Property. One day this will be your legacy. I hope more children will have financial literacy at a younger age so you can truly chase your passion when you become an adult, without being stuck in a 9 to 5 job.

INTRODUCTION

This book is about commercial property investment. It is written as a practical guide you can pick up and use, and contains all the foundational knowledge you need to get started in your commercial property journey. In addition to the basics, it covers strategy and understanding your big picture in order to work out your pathway. The book covers personal stories of deals I have done as well as ones from my clients, so you can find inspiration in situations like yours.

Further, I will take you through:

- the risks and rewards of commercial property investment
- making an offer
- structuring your investments
- calculating your yields and returns
- set and forget, uplift and growth property strategies
- investing via a self-managed super fund (SMSF)
- due diligence
- buying in different states around Australia
- client stories and much much more.

While this book was written as a journey from beginning to end you can also read the chapters that are of particular interest to you to give you a quick launch guide.

I view my job as a buyer's agent, and the job of my company, Unikorn Commercial Property, as building wealth for my clients, not just selling them a property, and this is how I have approached this book. It's about you, your individual journey and what you need to get there, and this is your guidebook.

Commercial property is the other side of the coin of property investment. It is the natural on-flow from a residential portfolio, giving you cash flow while your residential property gives you growth. But if you are starting out and want to know if you can start with commercial property and skip residential property altogether, you can use this book as your foundation to do that too.

I wrote this book to break down the myths and demystify the commercial property industry so everyday Australians like yourself can invest with confidence and security. All the information in this book is current at the time of writing. Bear that in mind, as the property market, both residential and commercial, will continue to evolve, grow and change. The possible returns detailed in this book may have all changed by the time you invest. However, the principles don't change; you just have to find a new returns benchmark in the industry when you are ready to invest.

If you are located overseas but looking to invest in Australia (or potentially looking to invest in commercial property in your local area or country), the principles and foundation of commercial property are the same no matter where you are buying it. What changes are the structures (e.g. investing through a company or trust or LLC) and the funding. Buying in different company structures varies from country to country, just like it varies from state to state in Australia based on how you want to manage your tax. And with funding, in the US for example you can easily get an 80 per cent loan on commercial property, whereas in New Zealand, loans on commercial property are for a maximum of 60 per cent.

If you are looking at investing in Australia from overseas, these principles and foundations apply and these examples are relevant to you. However, as an overseas investor, the loans and funding will be different and so will the structure that holds the property.

If you are looking to use this book as a tool for investing in other countries, terminology (such as cap rate, yield, etc.) will be different in other countries but the principles are the same.

Remember, learning is an ongoing endeavour. After finishing this book you can check out additional resources at cashedupcommercial.com.au or HelenTarrant.com so you can continue to learn, grow and invest. Alternatively, if you want to surround yourself with a good team of advisors on your commercial property journey, check out my company, Unikorn Commercial Property, and let us create your blueprint to financial freedom via commercial property.

Good luck! Your journey begins now...

CHAPTER 1

MY PATH TO COMMERCIAL PROPERTY

Most of the time when you hear someone speak on stage, or you read an inspiring autobiography, it's all about rags to riches: how someone's mum and dad have migrated on a boat, managing to survive with nothing, and now they're financially free. My story is a little bit different.

EARLY YEARS IN BEIJING

I grew up in the best part of China. I was born in Beijing, one street away from what would be equivalent today to Sydney's Pitt Street. The suburb is called WanFuJing. One of the most famous icons of the area is a big Catholic church, the first one to be built in China, that today has a big courtyard where the local residents sit, chat and dance in the evenings. My maternal grandparents had lived there for over 50 years, and this family home was where I was born and grew up. It was the only home I knew in China.

My family home was ten minutes' walk to Tiananmen Square and the Forbidden City. I went to preschool in the Royal Botanic

Gardens, next to the Forbidden City. Life was great. China after the cultural revolution was on a course for rapid growth and wealth. My grandparents were architects, and our whole family was in property — so even from a young age, property was in my blood.

In a communist country, you didn't have social mobility. This meant that if you wanted to become an entrepreneur or a business owner but you didn't have the connections, or your family was not in the trade, it was nigh on impossible.

Dad's family were revolutionaries. His parents had fought alongside Chairman Mao for the new China. My paternal grandfather was part of the team of accountants who worked out rations for the nation. My paternal grandmother joined the Red Army when she was 16. The party arranged their marriage.

My maternal grandparents were scared their family would get purged again in a new revolution, so they arranged the marriage of their only daughter (my mother) to a man from a strong revolutionary family so we would never be purged again.

Two significant events marked my birth year: the introduction of colour television, and the implementation of the one-child policy that was introduced in 1980. Since I was born in February 1981, I was one of the first batches of only children to be born under the new policy.

I started life pretty comfortably. I was an only child and the eldest of the only children, which meant that my grandparents and parents absolutely spoiled me! I had the best that life could give me in terms of attention and love — not money, because no-one actually earned much money in a communist country. Unless you had connections, you earned a normal wage.

My mother had a hobby sewing kids' clothing, because during her teenage years in the cultural revolution everything was grey, and she hated dark colours. So as soon as coloured fabric was available she would make me colourful clothing. (To this day I seldom wear black. I always wear bright, happy colours when I can.)

The only hiccup to growing up in Beijing was that the air quality was awful, and I developed chronic asthma before I was five. I was hospitalised almost monthly in winter and when the seasons changed. I was better in summer, but not during the hot days. I struggled to breathe, and my mother didn't know if I was going to survive childhood.

Back then, parents couldn't stay overnight with their child in hospital, so I stayed in a ward with five to six children all suffering the same illness. The hospital conditions were basic. They had so many cases of children with chronic asthma and were short-staffed most of the time, so if it wasn't an emergency, no-one would attend to you. My parents would be the last to leave and the first in the morning to line up outside the door to come in. If I was better by the next day I would run to the hospital door to greet them. If I was ill I would be lying in bed, coughing. One of my first memories was of my mother placing a bunch of bananas on my pillow above my head when she left the hospital one night. She told me if I was hungry in the middle of the night I could always feel for a banana without having to call for the nurses.

My mother couldn't sleep when I was in hospital, so she would watch TV through the night. They would air a lot of American movies during the middle of the night, so that's what my mother would watch.

One night, Mum was watching a movie called *10*. She had a light-bulb moment as she watched Bo Derek running along a beautiful beach. She knew if she could take me away from China to a seaside country, I would be able to be healthy again and have a better life. This light-bulb moment changed my life forever.

My mother was the eldest of four kids, and had three younger brothers. They each influenced my life in different ways when I was growing up, but that's a story for another day.

As luck would have it, one of my uncles met his future wife, the daughter of a diplomat, while working in a hotel for which my grandfather was the chief architect. She was half Chinese and half Russian. When her father finished his time at the Russian embassy, they migrated to Australia in 1986. My uncle followed, and in 1987 they were married in Sydney. A year later, my uncle asked my mother if she would like to join him in Sydney as he wanted some of his family nearby. To my mother it was the opportunity she was waiting for, but not without her daughter. She insisted that if she was to go to Australia she needed to take me with her.

LEAVING HOME

My parents sold everything they had to buy the tickets for me and my mother. My mother, at the age of 35, arrived in Sydney with her seven-year-old daughter, $70 and not a word of English. We started off living in Fairfield in Western Sydney, in my uncle's garage. My mother didn't know where she was and how she was going to realise her dreams. She had no real skill set and had a young child to raise. My uncle and aunt were expecting their first child, Veronica, and they expected Mum to look after their baby while they worked. My uncle became a bricklayer, and my aunt was a nurse. They paid Mum $50 per month and gave her board and food, although my mother had to do all the childcare, cooking and cleaning around the house.

Life was tough and totally different to what she expected. But Mum had me and we were going to make it work. My first hurdle was schooling. It took my mother three months to figure out how to get me into the local primary school. It was a 15- to 20-minute walk to school. In those days, Mum didn't know how to drive, so we walked everywhere. Mum used to put my cousin Veronica in a pram, and we would get groceries for the house and walk to the park on our path to and from school.

The highlight of my week was on Sundays, as an ice cream truck would come along. You know, the ones that play music and sell soft serve. My mother would buy me one every week as a treat, and to this day, if I see an ice cream truck in the suburbs or by the beach, I have to go and buy an ice cream!

Starting school was a challenge for me because I was smaller than the average child at school. By the time I went to school I started in year 3, as I was eight years old, but I looked like I should have been in year 1. I probably weighed 15 kilograms and was really short. I had a lot to catch up on, and I didn't speak English, but after three months I learned enough English to get by.

My father joined us a year later. He came on the last flight before the infamous Tiananmen Square massacre, and we were then stuck in Australia for the next seven years. We became residents due to the Bob Hawke amnesty, which is why to this day our family always votes for Labor at any election.

GETTING BY

Before my mother came to Australia she was a bookkeeper working for the Department of Housing. She didn't have any skills that were transferrable. When we came to Australia, my mother couldn't speak English so she read Chinese newspapers to try to find a job, and realised that she could get a job sewing because she used to make clothes for me. From then on we became a sweat shop. My mother made clothes for two big department stores and brand name labels, but was paid a pittance for each item, like $2.50 for a shirt that sold for well over $100. To this day I don't buy designer labels or brand name clothing because I know the workers who made them were never paid adequately for them. For me it's always been about value for money and substance (which is probably what my clients and community are attracted to).

During the peak season there was so much work to do that both my dad and I had to help out on the machines to meet deadlines. I would miss school because I would be on the machine overnight with Mum, finishing a job, and then be up while she slept to check over the quality before the work was picked up. In the low season we could barely make our rent. My father, who had been an electrician in China, worked long hours as a chef, then became a baker working the night shift after one of his colleagues bought a Bakers Delight franchise in Lane Cove.

We moved from one suburb and school to another. Cabramatta. Fairfield. Smithfield. Auburn. Waterloo, North Sydney, Chatswood, Roseville, Wahroonga. My mother was always looking for a better community where I could grow up with the right influences around me. In one three-year period we moved every year. I got very good at scooping up my belongings into black garbage bags and moving to the next house. It taught me to live in the now: to quickly adapt to a new environment and make friends, but never really put down roots. To appreciate the little things in life.

I remember when I was about 16 years old, one day my parents and our pets were all in the same lounge room having lunch (the only meal we could all have together due to our schedules). I realised that this was happiness for me, and at that moment I had everything

I needed in my life. To this day I always prefer a lunch meeting rather than dinner.

Wherever we moved, the sewing machines followed us (see figure 1.1, overleaf). My parents used to jokingly say they were my ONLY inheritance.

By the time my mother was in her late forties I was more independent and my mother felt she didn't need to be at home for me anymore, so she started a new career. She told me it was because when you hit your forties you need to move more otherwise your health will suffer. She went from working for someone as a kitchen hand to nannying, to cleaning and learning how to do professional massages.

My parents' sewing machines still sit in their garage today. They have a sentimental value for me, as when we moved we would always have to set up shop in a garage or in a spare room, and insulate the walls the best we could so our neighbours wouldn't know what we did. Growing up like that taught me about grounding, and a good work ethic, but also that no matter how hard you work, if you don't leverage or work smarter you are never going to get ahead.

This is why I am so passionate about changing peoples' lives through commercial property. My parents woke up in their late fifties and wanted a way to retire, but it was too late to invest and too late for them to change their skills. They'd be on the age pension and heading for a pretty ordinary retirement. Through commercial property, I found a way to accelerate the journey to financial freedom, effectively halve the investment time, and possibly get ten times more cash flow.

Helping my parents to have the retirement they deserve has been a mission of mine. I am determined to tick off my parents' bucket list before they get too old or too forgetful to enjoy it.

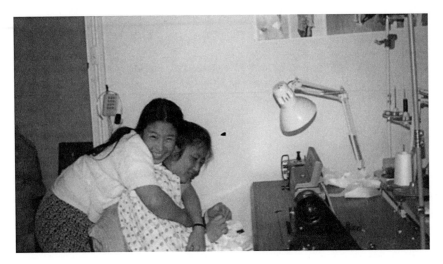

Figure 1.1: My mother and I at the sewing machine when I was 14 years old

MY FIRST CASH LESSONS

My parents always wanted to start their own business. For one crazy year when I was 14 we ran our own takeaway shop in Waverly, in the eastern suburbs of Sydney. We moved into the residence at the back, set up the sewing machines in the lounge area, and life started again. I went to a new school and tried to figure out how to help my parents run a takeaway shop. I'd never made a hamburger in my life but I am always open to new experiences.

This was my first experience with commercial property and leases, dealing with suppliers and trying to make a business work. I learned that cash flow is king when running a business. The takeaway business didn't survive and 12 months later we moved back to the north shore and I went back to my old school. It was sad for my parents but they had a go and we were all in it together, so it was just another adventure. When we got back to the north shore my mother stopped sewing and started work as a kitchen hand, while

Dad went back to being a baker and started working for Coles. Life started to be stable again.

I started working when I was almost 15 — 14 years and 9 months old, to be exact — in a library, and three nights a week waitressing in an Italian restaurant, all while studying at school through the day. I brought home $258 a week, which was a lot of money to me. I'll never forget the feeling I had the first time I was paid and able to contribute to the household.

When I started at university, I wanted my parents to buy a residential investment unit — I wanted them to finally start investing so they could eventually pay off their mortgage and, like everyone at the time, I thought this was the best way. When I told my parents they told my grandparents and everyone in my family was against it because they weren't comfortable with debt. I had to fight hard to get them to understand that, while they would be in debt, the tenants would help to pay down some interest and then allow them some capital growth. (That was back in the day when you were able to get good returns in residential property.)

I found a two-bedroom apartment in Crows Nest, on Sydney's north shore, for $251 000 in 2000. We struggled to keep it through the GFC, and eventually sold it for $560 000 in 2015. The sale of the unit helped my parents to pay down some of their mortgage, but it didn't give them financial freedom. I realised in that moment that even if you paid down all your debts and owned your home outright, you still needed cash flow to live: to pay the strata fees and the council rates, and be able to travel and eat. Having money in the bank and using capital wasn't the answer since inflation and longer life spans mean there is a real risk of outliving your capital; neither was having residential investments where the return was net 1 to 2 per cent, no different to putting it in the bank, and you'd have to sell in order to have the money to fund your lifestyle, meaning you weren't building generational wealth. I had to find a better solution if I wanted to help my parents in their retirement.

MAKING MY PARENTS PROUD

When I was 16, my mother told me that she couldn't financially provide the things I wanted in life, and that if I wanted them, I had to go out and get them on my own. For her it was heartbreaking to tell her child that. For me it was liberating because I knew that I could chart my own path. I felt she had set me free. I wasn't sure what I wanted to do with my life, but knew I wanted to run my own national company. And I knew I wanted to make my parents proud. I wanted them to have all the experiences in life they missed out on because they chose to bring me to Australia.

One of my biggest life lessons was that just because everyone else has low expectations of you doesn't mean that you should have them for yourself. My extended family never thought I would go to university because I was a girl — and an attractive girl — and they wanted me to just marry someone who was well off. So I thought I would do a trade at TAFE, because I thought I wasn't smart enough for university.

However, when I got 85.9 on my HSC score, I thought the world had given me a second chance. I ended up getting into a Commerce degree at Macquarie University. After around 18 months of studying and finding out what made Asian parents proud, I transferred to a combined degree in Law and Business, majoring in Marketing. That meant five years of study, followed by two years of college Law so I could practise.

With all the demands on my time with my studies, seven years of waitressing three nights a week was not an option. So I began searching for something else I could do to support my studies, and I found beauty therapy. My mother always wanted me to have a trade that I could fall back on if need be, so beauty therapy and having my own salon seemed a good idea when I was 22. I bought a single operator salon in Narrabeen and hired a beauty therapist while I took different beauty courses to qualify myself. Two years later, I opened another salon in Gordon and a store at Parklea Markets, and hired more staff. I was juggling a long commute to study at night and work in the salon in the day, and I read marketing and advertising books during my free time at the salon. I worked seven days a week and had a packed schedule. I thought I had my life figured out.

STARTING OUT IN RESIDENTIAL INVESTMENT

Like most people, my first investments were in residential property. There was lots of information out there and courses I could take and I started implementing them right away. My aim was always cash flow. When you have migrant parents and are self-employed, you realise how important cash flow is. I was earning money and saving as much as I could for a deposit on a property. I couldn't afford to buy in Sydney. So I looked further afield — around Gosford — and discovered an older suburb called Koolewong, which had water views from elevated positions. So I bought the worst house in the best street. The property had two two-bedroom units, upstairs and downstairs, and separate meters. I thought of it as my backup plan: if things went wrong, my parents and I would still have a place to live. In the meantime I planned to renovate it and rent it out and keep it as an investment.

I paid $325 000 for it and lived in the property while I renovated. Six months later I put a tenant in. Various tenants came and went, but one was a big problem: always behind in her rent, always issues. Her 17-year-old son broke windows and painted graffiti on the walls. It was a nightmare. It cost me $20 000 to evict that tenant and patch up the property.

That was a huge learning curve about residential property investment, because you don't always get the best tenants and there are so many little earthquakes that can chew up your cash flow. Every time I thought I had some cash flow, I had to get a water heater, an air conditioner or a sliding door replaced. It would cost $6000 to just remove a tree from the backyard ... and it goes on and on.

I couldn't see how I was going to be financially free in a short space of time by repeating this strategy, so I was keen to try different residential investment strategies for cash flow. I went regional because that was what the 'gurus' said would give you the positive cash flow you needed. I went to Armidale because I was studying at the University of New England doing a Psychology degree at the time. (When I finished my Law degree I wanted to do something for myself and I had always wanted to study Psychology because when I had my salon I was fascinated by all my clients' stories and the emotions and psychology behind it. I never wanted to practise ... I just wanted to learn.) At UNE (before online learning) we had seven- to ten-day intensives where you had to study at the university. I would stay in town at a motel, and in my spare time I would walk around the town and look at properties.

At the time you could get properties in Armidale for under $200 000 that delivered good cash flow. With some equity from my Koolewong property, and my own savings, I bought my first property in Armidale for $180 000, grossing 9 per cent, but with property management fees, rates, outgoings and my mortgage,

I still only made around $100 a week. For most people that would be a pretty good return for a residential property. But for me it didn't seem enough. I continued to build my portfolio and bought another property in Armidale a year later, just ten minutes' walk to the university. The sale price was $210 000 and rental income was $275 a week. Not quite $100 a week for me with this property, but I considered $70 to $80 a week still good cash flow for residential.

Despite my residential cash flow with three properties, I was now deposit and serviceability tapped out so I couldn't buy any more. I needed to either save faster, earn more or find a better cash flow option. If you are reading this book, you may be at this point if you have invested in residential property up until now. For me this realisation hit home, big time.

I'd had high hopes of a big property portfolio to help my parents retire, and those hopes were dashed. There was no way they could retire on my $170 a week of residential property income. I needed at least $50 000 a year in cash flow.

THE COMMERCIAL LIGHTBULB MOMENT

In my salon in Narrabeen, I paid $400 a week in rent. I opened the business from Tuesdays to Saturdays. It took the first two days to pay my rent. On Thursdays I could pay for stock. Fridays were for tax. It was only on Saturdays when I could make any profit. But Saturdays were the busiest, and so I made the best profits. Most people around me were doing the same type of thing. The massage therapist. The hairdresser.

Bill, the landlord, was heading for retirement. He used to collect the rent and then go fishing. His income from our rent and the two tenants upstairs meant he could live the life he loved. And that got me thinking.

I started my research into commercial property investment. I checked with the local café. The laundromat. The coffee shop and the bakery, all the small business owners along the strip where I had my salon. They worked hard, took care of their premises, and paid the rent on time. So different from my experience with residential tenants.

Cue my light-bulb moment. Maybe I should look into commercial property. Could that get me to financial freedom? But me being me, I researched. I did my due diligence. I looked at leases and talked to the local agency. I began to look at things from a different viewpoint, and glimpsed the potential of commercial property. What if you could halve your investment journey time and make ten times as much cash flow investing in commercial than in residential??

MY FIRST COMMERCIAL PROPERTY

It was 2012 when I bought my first commercial property. I'd seen the potential of commercial property, but I didn't know how to start. I knew that in a time of stress, people will sell their cash flow properties to hold onto their growth properties. But if the market's down they won't buy growth properties.

Just like any investor starting out, I wanted a property within driving distance. (In hindsight, in the nine years since I've had my first commercial property, I've seen the property twice. However, when you first start it seems so important.) So I looked in Sydney for an affordable commercial property and found a Japanese restaurant of 55 square metres in North Sydney, at the end of an arcade. It was advertised at $395 000, and that was my price point. So I went there for a meal, and to watch customers come and go. It was very busy, with people coming in for lunch. And the food was excellent.

In 2012 if you were to buy residential property it would give you about a 5 to 6 per cent gross return (before outgoings and mortgage). The biggest difference is commercial property is worked on net yields: the rental yield is quoted after outgoings but before the mortgage. (The reason the mortgage is not included in the calculation is because everyone's mortgage is different.) However, outgoings are known in commercial property, and a commercial property is always sold on the net yield. When comparing the North Sydney restaurant to an apartment the difference was crazy. If I took the outgoings out of the residential apartment, my net yield would be around 2 to 3 per cent compared to 8 per cent in this commercial property. At first I thought that I was missing something — why hadn't anyone told me about this before? I thought it was too good to be true. As it turns out, all my clients say the same thing even now when they buy their first commercial property.

When I realised the cash flow you can generate on a commercial property it was a big awakening. At that time the interest rate for commercial was 6 per cent, which meant I'd clear around $10 000 a year in positive cash flow.

After we did an inspection, the agent, who couldn't have been less interested in me, handed me a contract and told me the vendor had decided to sell at $360 000 to the first person to exchange contracts, and that there was another person interested. The agent also told me that the vendor was a solicitor himself and resided in the same building. It was now or never. The numbers on paper stacked up, but I didn't look at the outgoings. I didn't know what else to ask.

I knew nothing about commercial property contracts, and time was running out. I went to at least five legal firms until I found one who could see the contract right away. The minute the contract was signed, I was in my car and drove to North Sydney in record time. I even parked in a No Standing zone. If my car was towed, it would be worth it. I ran in my heels for ten minutes to get to the vendor's office, and I was totally puffed out when I arrived at the front desk. I was ushered into the boardroom, where the wait seemed forever, even though it was probably only a few minutes.

It was the longest 15 minutes of my life, watching the vendor carefully check the contract. He even called the bank to verify that I had money there to clear the cheque I gave him. When the vendor finally accepted the contract, I heaved a sigh of relief. It was done. When I walked out of the vendor's office, the other purchaser was sitting in the foyer with contract in hand. I had beaten him by just ten minutes.

Then I called the agent. He was very polite, thinking that I was going to tell him I was on my way to the vendor. But he was stunned into silence when I told him that I'd just exchanged contracts on the North Sydney property. He'd thought I was an outsider who had no chance of getting the property.

I held that North Sydney property for nine years before selling it for $1 050 000. It was an emotional decision, but it was the right one to make, because there were bigger properties out there to buy.

A UNIKORN IS BORN

When I bought my first commercial property the industry was like a secret club for high-income earners and high-level professionals. I was empowered to go out and educate everyday Australians on commercial property because I believe that everyone deserves to have a choice to invest in commercial property or residential (and to be truly successful you should have both in your portfolio).

I started educating everyday Australians on commercial property in 2016. During the first years of my commercial investment journey there were no education courses, no books relating to the Australian market; I learned through trial and error, and it was a massive learning curve. I used a lot of the residential property strategies in commercial and realised the multiplier effect was larger.

My husband and I started buying in Sydney in 2012 to 2014. We leveraged pretty hard, and didn't really look into different owner-ship structures. Our strategy was mainly focused on cash flow but we also did vacant and uplift strategies where we manufactured growth and then sold and bought again. We started going into regional areas in 2014 as the yields in the metro cities started to drop. We also bought in Melbourne and in regional Victoria. In 2016 we started to buy into Queensland.

I learned a lot about managing debt, structuring our portfolio, and the three stages of wealth creating (leverage, tweak and maintain, consolidation — these are now the stages of investment I take my clients through).

Today I am still the only educator teaching everyday Australians how to invest in commercial property. I feel that there are more pitfalls in commercial property than residential and that you really need to understand the foundations before you invest. This is why I am so big on education and I have so much free content out there on my YouTube channel and podcasts.

Once I started to get traction with my education program, my students would ask me to look for a property for them. At the time I didn't know if I could do it, so I started with a handful of students on a trial program. When I realised I could deliver value and that I could help my clients achieve passive income and financial freedom in a short space of time using my strategies I started becoming a buyer's agent. This was in late 2017 before the commercial property industry had even heard of buyer's agents. Since 2017 my business has doubled almost every year, mainly from referrals and previous clients and my YouTube channel. I started launching group deals and syndicates in 2020, just before the pandemic. Again this was driven by the demand of my clients who wanted to do larger deals and access things such as childcare centres and petrol stations and storage facilities. I then started putting clusters of clients into investor pods for them to be able to invest in larger and larger deals together so they can get higher yields. Now, Unikorn Commercial Property has three services: education, a buyer's agency and syndicates.

Today, just as I fought for my first commercial property, I fight for every single one of our clients as a buyer's agent. Helping everyday Aussies purchase commercial cash flow properties is what I live and breathe. I gave up my dream of sitting on the beach doing nothing to work 16-hour days changing people's lives via commercial property and I wouldn't have it any other way. What gets me up in the morning is knowing that every day I make an impact in someone's life that they will never forget. I help them to be financially free sooner and better.

FINAL THOUGHTS

I learned to invest in commercial property the hard way, through trial and error. There were deals where I could have negotiated harder, done my due diligence better, monitored the agent better and replaced the tenants sooner. The list goes on. I lost money on some, on others I broke even, and some I made windfalls on. I have been investing in commercial property for ten years now, and I believe I've cracked the code on commercial property. I have well and truly had my 10 000 hours. Today I am a wiser investor, but I have also learned to look at each and every deal through the eyes of my investor clients so I can find the perfect deal for them. The market doesn't get easier. You have to get better. It's a mindset game. Every time I think I can't find the stock or the yields for my clients, I tell myself I have to do better, work harder and go deeper so I can be better and do better.

My mission is to make the commercial property industry accessible to everyday Australians, and to educate people on and demystify commercial property to create the shortest pathway to financial freedom. My clients motivate me to be the best in the commercial industry. For me, every deal I do for my clients is a personal one, because that's the only way I can truly help another person create financial freedom.

CHAPTER 2
WHY COMMERCIAL PROPERTY?

In your property investment journey you need to balance cash flow with growth. Residential is primarily about growth and commercial about cash flow. Ideally you need both in your portfolio because, if you chase growth, eventually you will run out of capacity to service the debt so you won't be able to continue to buy. This is usually once you own about three properties, if you're lucky. But if you only chase cash flow, you'll run out of equity to leverage against for the next deposit. Only when you have a balance of growth and cash flow properties in your portfolio can you continue to buy and create a faster journey to financial freedom.

Normally you start your property journey with residential, and you tend to keep going until you have maxed out your capacity. If your wages continue to grow each time you use the equity of your residential property, it may be some years before you realise you need a cash flow property to support your growth properties.

We start out with the misconception that we need to financially support our own portfolio as it grows, while the truly wealthy actually set up their portfolio, then let it sustain itself as soon as possible. Let me explain.

When you buy a residential property the income from the property isn't enough to pay all the outgoings plus the mortgage; typically you will need to take money out of your pocket every week to support it. This may be small, like $20 or $50 per week, but eventually after you buy a few properties it tends to add up. When you have to support your property portfolio like this, it depends on you; this means if something happens to you, if you lose your job or if you fall ill, then you will struggle to sustain it.

With commercial the aim is that you start building positive cash flow so the portfolio is self-supporting. This means that if something happens to you the property would be fine — in fact, it may be able to support you if you are out of work or ill. However, you need to balance your portfolio always with growth and cash flow so you can continue to grow and leverage.

WHEN YOU BUY RESIDENTIAL

If you bought a residential investment property in Sydney or Melbourne in the last few years, you would most likely have paid around $2 million for that property. Your tenant is paying you rent at about $1000 per week to live in a great suburb in your property, and you're subsidising their lifestyle by $20 000 a year — out of your own pocket. On a $2 million property, your loan would most likely be around $1.5 million, with interest on the loan around $50 000. Then add council rates, water and sewerage rates, insurance and management fees, as well as maintenance of the property, which could be an extra $5000 per year. So, all in all you won't be able to afford too many of these properties if you have to spend $400 per week to support it.

Since the 1950s, Australian residential property has doubled every seven to nine years, which means that your $2 million property, in seven to nine years, will likely be worth somewhere around

$4 million. This may be hard to imagine right now, but you might have $2 million of equity that you could draw down over the next seven to nine years. The only problem is that you can't access that equity, because your wages won't grow fast enough in the same time, and if you have to shell out $400 per week to support that property, you won't be able to buy many before you are unable to service them.

In the last two years, right after people got over the pandemic, property prices soared in the metro cities. We've seen double-digit growth in many suburbs around Sydney, Melbourne and Brisbane. This means that if you had your $2 million property, it's now worth $2.4 million, which means you've made $400 000, which is really great. The maximum a bank would lend you on that money is 80 per cent. You may be thinking, 'Well, with that extra $320 000 I could potentially access, that could be part of a deposit to buy a million-dollar commercial property.'

The problem is that your wages didn't go up by 20 per cent to 40 per cent in the last two years. In fact, most people were lucky to have even kept their jobs. Others have had to take a pay cut, and most wouldn't have had a pay increase over that time. The reality is that your $400 000 is now trapped in your property and you cannot get access to it unless you sell (which has all sorts of tax implications) or get a minimum 20 per cent increase in your wage.

This is the common scenario we see at Unikorn Commercial Property with our clients every day. They have accumulated a great growth portfolio with lots of equity. But equity doesn't feed their kids or pay for holidays. They can't draw down on it and they can't use it. They don't want to sell because of tax implications, so they're stuck.

We spend a lot of time working out strategies for these clients by unlocking their equity step by step as we build cash flow into their portfolio to make it more balanced, eventually becoming a cash flow portfolio when they head to retirement.

WHEN YOU BUY COMMERCIAL

A tenanted commercial property can give you a positive cash flow from day one, if done right. Plus, each year a rental increase is built into the property lease. Every year on the anniversary of the lease, the property rent increases by the minimum of the Consumer Price Index, but usually around 3 per cent or more, depending on your lease. This means that not only is more cash flow coming into your pocket, but it also insulates you against interest rate rises.

Commercial property leases are usually three to five years, or even seven years. Sometimes medical tenants (on lower yields) will sign up on ten-year leases. Tenants also often have additional options to renew at the end of their lease, which allows them to stay even longer in your premises.

The other great thing about commercial is that your tenant takes care of your property as if it's their own, because it's their livelihood. Whether they have a fish and chip shop, a restaurant or a dental surgery, a gym or an office for their business headquarters, commercial tenants need their premises to look slick and beautiful for when their customers and clients visit them. Ultimately it's where your tenant's livelihood is derived, so they have an additional incentive to take care of it. Most Australians actually spend more time in their work premises over the span of their working lives than in their own homes, so most commercial tenants want to make their premises a place they want to go to.

Over the time they are in your premises, a commercial tenant will also add value to your property. For example, if your tenant needs disability access, they might build a disability ramp. If your tenant is a gym, and they need to put in their own showers and toilets, they'll put them in (with your permission and maybe some contribution depending on your lease agreement).

Your tenants will often improve the value of your property as they stay there for the long term. And, from a value and market point of view, the longer your tenant stays in your premises, the more of a stable history they establish, so your property will be worth more. One thing for sure is that your commercial tenants won't be asking you to unblock their toilets or fix a leaking tap — that is their responsibility.

BALANCING YOUR PORTFOLIO FOR CASH FLOW AND GROWTH

As you build your portfolio, you need to balance buying cash flow properties and growth properties. This way, as the cash flow grows in your cash flow properties, you can use it to access more equity to buy again. You can also use your cash flow properties to support your lifestyle — pay for holidays, school fees, car payments, renovations, and to support your growth properties so you don't have to sell them if you lose your job or become ill.

Every time you buy a growth property, you should buy a cash flow property to follow. For example, if you buy a $500 000 residential property as your starter property, you should follow that with a cash flow commercial property either at the same price point or higher.

If, in the next seven to nine years, your residential property doubles to $1 million, technically you have 80 per cent of that equity to draw down to buy new properties, which is about $400 000. But you won't be able to access that equity gain unless you have additional cash flow. So as your property goes from $500 000 to $750 000 in, say, three years' time, you should be drawing down on the additional equity to buy a commercial property for around $500 000 that can give you around $15 000 in positive cash flow each year.

If you're the average Australian earning between $70 000 and $80 000 per year, a $15 000 cash flow after all expenses and mortgage means an 18 to 21 per cent increase in your income. This means you will be able to show the bank your income plus the $15 000 in cash flow, plus any of the rent from your residential investments. In a few years' time, you can take the income generated by your commercial property plus your residential property to access the equity on both properties to buy again.

Whether you buy residential or commercial as your third property really depends on what your big picture goals are. If you want growth, you can still be in commercial — but residential will always give you more growth than commercial. When it comes to cash flow though, nothing beats commercial property!

Figure 2.1 is a diagram of what your portfolio should aim to look like.

No matter what stage you are at in your investing journey, it's important to continue to grow your portfolio. You can only do that if you have a combination of growth and cash flow properties. This is why it's important to have both residential and commercial properties in your portfolio. You owe it to yourself to continuously grow that portfolio, along with your cash flow, so that you can continue to invest. You cannot afford to sit out for five years.

A lot of people wrongly think that just because the market is going up or the interest rate is going up, that they should sit out on a deal for a while. That's the wrong assumption. Yes, interest rates will go up. We may have another pandemic. Or another war. However,

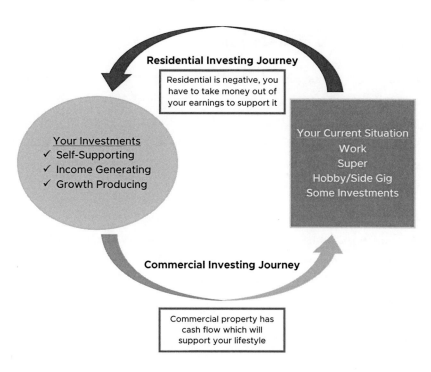

Figure 2.1: example portfolio

at the end of the day, with more people now entering the property market, a small change in the interest rate is not going to dent the buying frenzy.

As an investor, my attitude has always been to prepare to fight for the deals. Fight for your property, but also be prepared to pay just a little more — within reason and returns — because today's expensive is tomorrow's cheap.

If you plan to hold a property for any more than two years, then a slight compromise on yield or price point will be made up in rental increases in years to come. If you wait now to see what happens in the market, you'll get a lower return than if you'd got into the market six to 12 months before. You can never beat time in the market, so the time to go is now.

CREATE GENERATIONAL WEALTH

To create true generational wealth, you need to keep managing your portfolio so you buy and sell at the right time in different markets, either refinancing or selling when each property has hit its peak, so you can gradually move further up the ladder to buy bigger and better properties.

To prepare a strategy for long-term wealth, you need to have knowledge of both residential and commercial property, coupled with life experience and an in-depth understanding of tax implications and legal implications. Creating a blueprint and a pathway is what I love about working with my clients. From the beginning, there should be three phases to your investment journey:

1. acceleration
2. tweaks and maintenance
3. consolidation.

ACCELERATION

Typically, during this stage you want to leverage and borrow from the bank as much as possible. This is because you want to reach a certain level of income and asset base. For many people it's scary to have so much debt. But it's not forever. It's about buying value and investing in cash flow, which ultimately will get you to the next level. If you're starting out in commercial, this is when you need a lot of help, so aligning yourself with the right team of mentors, buyer's agents, accountants, lawyers and finance brokers is the right way to make sure you are going through the acceleration stage with confidence and security.

This is the time when you leverage as much as possible. It's the time where you try to find as many deposits as you can. When I first started in commercial property in 2012, I just looked for deposits everywhere, refinancing and selling my residential properties, getting my husband to sell shares in a company, using equity from our family home, selling my business and even borrowing from my family. I was on a pathway from 2014 to 2016 to accumulate as much commercial property as I could get my hands on.

TWEAKS AND MAINTENANCE

Not every property you get will be a great property. But the important thing to remember is the property ownership journey is about taking a good property and making it great during the time you own it.

Once you have gone through the acceleration stage of your property journey, you have leveraged yourself up with a few properties. The next step is to make a plan for improving every one of your properties. This might be tweaking the rent on the properties. Or it could be doing some cosmetic refurbishments so you can increase the value or attract a better tenant. Some improvements may require an extension or the creation of more lettable areas so you can charge more rent.

Ultimately this stage is about making your property great, and getting the maximum value out of it. This could take as little as a year, but usually allow two to three years. It doesn't mean that you can't buy during that time if you want to. You can always refinance one of your properties to keep buying. But I usually take this time to take stock of what I have, re-evaluate my plans and get my portfolio performing as best it can.

CONSOLIDATION

This is typically the phase where you cash out from your portfolio. It can be approached in two ways:

1. Sell off some of your accumulated assets, because they've reached their maximum value for you, so you can go from a starter property to a larger property.

2. Cash out towards retirement and only hold on to some key assets.

Many people think that once they buy a property, they should hold on to it forever. That's not correct. It's just like a starter house in residential real estate. Once you've extracted the full value of it for you, you should sell it and upgrade to the next house.

REAL-LIFE EXAMPLES

A prime example is my first commercial property. It was a tiny restaurant of 55 square metres in North Sydney, at the end of an arcade with Aldi, Oporto and some other cafes. When I bought the property, I knew nothing about commercial property except that it was $360 000 and yielding 8 per cent.

Over the years that I held this property, I ran market appraisals and raised the rent to keep it in line with the market. That kept the property performing at peak level.

I sold that property nine years later in June 2021 for $1 050 000. It was an extremely emotional sale for me because it was my first ever commercial property and I thought I would keep it forever. But at the end of the day, I sold it for 5 per cent yield, and I had extracted all the value out of that property in both cash flow and growth. Furthermore, with the money from the sale I could buy a $2 million property in a fringe or regional area for a higher than 5 per cent yield and have a larger footprint. I could go to Townsville and buy a freestanding property at 7 per cent or go to Brisbane and buy a 6 per cent yielding retail property. Either way, with the sale of my first property, I upgraded to a larger, more value-driven property.

If your property has already made leaps and bounds for you over the years — and it can be over two to three years or as many as ten or 15 years — there is a time to sell. (I discuss this more in chapter 13.)

Another example of growing your portfolio is a client of mine who I placed into a property on the Sunshine Coast in early 2020, before the pandemic hit. He bought it for $900 000 at 7.2 per cent yield. In March 2022, in the same area just a few streets away, a similar property listed at 5 per cent at $1.2 million.

If I was that client, I would sell the property and take my 33 per cent capital gain, which is $300 000, plus my original deposit of a similar amount, and leverage up to a $1.7 million to $2 million property elsewhere. This could be an office space in Melbourne at 5.5 per cent yield (before the pandemic the standard yield in Melbourne was 4 per cent, but office spaces are not the favourite currently due to COVID, which means there is an opportunity for you make a gain ahead of the market coming back). Alternatively, they could reinvest the money into a regional freestanding property yielding 6 per cent, holding income with the ability to manufacture equity and increase rental return in the future. I would make some minor changes to increase the value of the property and then sit back and wait. In three to five years, if my new property has grown in value, then I could sell or refinance the property to pull out more equity for the next deal.

Table 2.1 (overleaf) shows you how much the market has moved in the same area over two years.

Table 2.1: Warana, QLD, warehouse property January 2020 vs March 2022

Date	January 2020	March 2022
Asking price	$900 000	$1 296 000
Net rent	$64 800	$64 800
Yield rate	7.2%	5%

As you can see, the value of warehouse property has grown on the Sunshine Coast, with over 40 per cent growth over a two-year period even with the rent staying the same (to take into account COVID's downward pressure on rent). Even for an incoming purchaser buying at a 5 per cent yield, they will still get capital growth as well as cash flow even buying in the present market.

MINIMISING RISK

Since we are talking about growing your portfolio, we need to discuss de-risking your portfolio at the same time. It is easy to leverage, and many investors often invest blindly because it's the trend to do so in a certain area, or for certain types of properties.

These investors pay a premium to buy into what the market perceives as 'secure' at the time. However, every property, whether residential or commercial, has its cycle. So while office space is not the favourite at the moment, and everyone wants to buy warehouses, in a few years that trend will change. This is why as you leverage, you need to also de-risk your portfolio, changing the spread of your investments across different states and property types so you can capture different property cycles in different states.

A good example of de-risking your portfolio is when some of our clients bought properties in Townsville between 2017 and 2019 for between 8 and 9 per cent yields — before the pandemic. Today, in 2022, the yield is around 7 per cent and 6 per cent for more established tenants (as the value of the property goes up the yield goes down — this is explained more in chapter 3). These clients would be better to sell now at 7 per cent and take the gains made in the last few years. In their situation, they could de-risk their portfolio by selling one of their Townsville properties and buying a metro property.

If you bought a commercial property in Townsville in 2017 for $700 000 to $800 000, today that property is worth around $1 million or more. Around a 30 per cent capital gain. If you sell it, you'll get back your deposit, plus the 30 per cent gain, which would give you a deposit of around $500 000 to buy your next property, like the following examples in metro.

In March 2022 we helped one of our clients to secure a $1.35 million property in Warriewood on the Sydney northern beaches. It was a skin cancer specialist clinic on a ten-year lease at a 5.3 per cent yield. While this is not a 7 per cent yielding property, a Sydney property will always outperform other states in capital growth over time; plus, Sydney properties are also the most secure due to natural demographic growth and demand. So if you were looking to de-risk your portfolio and buy something more secure after you have owned a regional property, then something like this property would be an ideal choice.

If you prefer Melbourne over Sydney, Unikorn in May 2022 secured a $1.2 million office property in Ringwood at a 5.75 per cent yield on a five-year lease to a finance and accounting company. Again, great location, great tenants and good long-term security. There are lower yields but it will have long-term capital growth and stability. A metro property will always be lower risk than a regional property. A larger property with multiple tenants will always be more secure than a single tenant, and having multiple properties is always more advisable than a single commercial property. You are at your highest risk when you have one commercial property. The moment you have two you have halved your risk, and the moment you don't have any tenants that are more than 25 per cent of your total rental income the more secure you are going to feel.

FINAL THOUGHTS

As I sign off for this chapter, all I have to say is the time to go into commercial property is now. The longer you wait the lower your yield. So, start now, no matter how small.

Once you start, make sure you have a good solid strategy, and mentor and team behind you so you know the right direction to move.

Finally, when you look at your overall portfolio, look at the macro situation across the country. Don't become totally focused on just one state and one type of property. To maximise your gains over time, you need to move and grow your portfolio over different states and different property types.

CHAPTER 3

COMMERCIAL PROPERTY VS RESIDENTIAL PROPERTY

In this chapter I will highlight the fundamental differences between commercial and residential property, and how, in order to be truly successful, you will need to have both in your portfolio so you can keep growing it. You need to invest in commercial for cash flow and residential for growth. Where investors go wrong is that they invest in residential property for cash flow and spend all their time trying to make it cash flow positive. Likewise, others invest in commercial and they want exponential growth while they have massive positive cash flow. Commercial has always been a cash flow strategy. And yes, there will be growth (as with all properties), but the growth in commercial fluctuates way more than residential because it's dependent on the type of tenant you put into the premises. So balancing residential and commercial is the best way to grow your wealth in the long term.

Regardless of whether you choose to invest in commercial property or in residential property after reading this book, I want you to think of property investment in terms of return on investment (ROI).

ROI: COMMERCIAL VS RESIDENTIAL

In my seminars, I would always ask the audience, 'If you are losing or negative in your cash flow, how much return do you want in capital growth to make a residential deal worthwhile?' The answer was always between 5 and 10 per cent, with almost the whole room agreeing that they would be happy with 10 per cent growth on their property per year if the cash flow was negative. So let's explore commercial property vs residential property in terms of ROI.

In every property investment there is cash flow and growth. You have to look at the big picture to know which is a better option for you. With commercial, you have more control over your portfolio than residential, because the cash flow is upfront and you know the figures when you buy the property. (Chapter 5 covers cash flow in more detail.) The growth of your commercial property is linked to the rental growth, plus market growth. (Refer to chapter 6 on growth for a detailed explanation.) In residential, you need to rely solely on market growth to make the investment work, even if that means losing some cash flow at the front end. See table 3.1.

Table 3.1: ROI on residential vs commercial property

ROI — metro properties	Residential property	Commercial property
Cash flow	−1%	5%
Growth	10%	5%
Total ROI	9%	10%
ROI — regional properties	Residential property	Commercial property
Cash flow	2%	7%
Growth	6%	4%
Total ROI	8%	11%

Ultimately, when you invest in property, you want to make sure you are getting the right returns on your money, and that you can compare those returns with other investment vehicles to see if you're getting the best leverage with your money.

The other thing to consider in any investment is the opportunity cost. Most investors don't think about this. They don't realise that if the equity is stuck in their investments, regardless of whether they are commercial or residential, that inflation will erode the value of their deposit. What you can buy today with a $100 000 deposit is a lot less than you could have bought two years ago, and two years before that. After reading this chapter, I want you to think about the true return of the deposit that you have previously invested into your property portfolio, and what you can do to maximise it.

CASH FLOW

There are many benefits of investing in commercial property, but the main one that people want is more cash flow — something they don't truly have with residential property.

RESIDENTIAL CASH FLOW

I speak to a lot of investors and many tell me that their residential property has a positive cash flow. They are very proud of this, although it could have taken them anywhere from five to ten years to get to the point where their residential property gives them cash flow. The problem is that they don't realise that all these years they've had no return on investment for the deposit they put into the property. Let me explain.

True positive cash flow is when your property pays for the interest repayment on both the deposit, the loan, and all the outgoings, and then gives you money on top of that. It is NOT when you have paid down your debt and you are getting positive cash flow. Nor is it when you are positive after taking out just the interest repayments on the loan itself.

For example, if you are buying a $500 000 metro residential property, the likely scenario is that you will need to put in 20 per cent deposit plus costs. With the deposit around $100 000, the loan is $400 000. Working on an interest rate of 4.5 per cent, the interest on the $400 000 would be $18 000 per year.

Your rent on a $500 000 property—which would be a one- or two-bedroom unit—is likely to be at most $450 per week, so that's $23 400 for full tenancy.

I have listed all your outgoings in table 3.2. As you'll see, when you take out your mortgage repayments, you're in the negative.

Table 3.2: residential investment property numbers

Annual rent	$23 400
Council fees	–$1000
Insurance	–$500
Water	–$1000
Management fees (7%)	–$1638
Maintenance (plumbers, electricians, etc.)	–$500
Interest on loan (4.5%)	–$18 000
Strata fees	–$8000
Cash flow	–$7238 negative cash flow
Annual return on $100 000 deposit	–7.2 per cent

If you manage to get a slight positive cash flow (under $1000) most investors have the misconception that they have a positive cash flow property. In actual fact they don't because they have forgotten to calculate the cost of their deposit. When you buy your first residential property you are most likely using a cash deposit, and then going forward you may or may not be using equity. There is an opportunity cost to your deposit, and even if it is cash, still around 1 per cent even at extremely low interest rates. So if you take in the cost of servicing your deposit the 'profit' is wiped out.

Even if we take that out of consideration, a $1000 or less per year return on the $100 000 they have put into the property is a 1 per cent (or less) return, which is worse than if you put the money in the bank! If the interest rate goes up, or if you have higher maintenance costs, then you're in negative territory. This means you are losing money on the front end in the hope you will make more, ideally double-digit capital growth, on the back end. I'll discuss capital growth in more detail later in this chapter.

A major difference between residential and commercial is that in residential you are subsidising your tenant's lifestyle, while in commercial the tenant is paying for your lifestyle.

Let me illustrate this.

In residential, if you buy a $1 million apartment right now it will be in a nice suburb and have amenities, such as a pool, gym, BBQ and grassed land area. It will have well-kept gardens and lifts, and be convenient to shops. Your tenant can live there for around $600 to $750 per week without worrying about paying the outgoings. They can just enjoy the lifestyle. In the meantime, you are going to work to pay for the negative gearing or shortfall between the mortgage and outgoings and the rent your tenant is paying. So, in essence, you are subsidising your tenant's lifestyle.

As prices grow, rents don't keep up with the rate of growth. Assume that you bought a house for $500 000 and next year it increases by 10 per cent. It would then be worth $550 000. But your rent wouldn't increase by 10 per cent. In fact, it may even remain stable, because there may not be enough demand in the market for that rental property. Even if it does go up, it's not in proportion to your outlays, because your outgoings also go up. For a residential investment property, you pay all the outgoings, and have to deal with increased council rates and special levies, in addition to the normal rates and insurance.

Let's say that you rented that property out for $350 a week. Next year, you might be able to raise it by $20 (5.5 per cent) a week to $370. But that rent did not grow by 10 per cent like the value of your property has. As your property value rises, the percentage return on your investment, your cash flow, actually lowers. It's an inverse relationship. As a residential investor, you are really waiting for the big capital gain of $50 000, $100 000 or $200 000.

COMMERCIAL CASH FLOW

In commercial, the calculations are done all on net yields. This can be confusing when a first-time investor enters the market. The first thing our clients, when they are coming from a residential background, want to know about a property is the outgoings so they can calculate if they can afford it. Sometimes we have to point out on the lease the fact that the tenant pays for all outgoings and we can see the mental shift — that aha! moment when they realise that they no longer have to worry about budgeting to have cash flow to pay all the outgoings.

The tenant pays all the outgoings — council rates, water rates, body corporate, insurance and sometimes even land tax — because your tenant is running their business in your premises. And that means less money out of your pocket, so more cash is flowing to you. Everything in commercial is reduced to a net rent. If your tenant pays $40 000 net rent plus outgoings and GST, and the outgoings are $10 000, it's the same as if your tenant is paying $50 000 gross rent plus GST ($40 000 net rent plus $10 000 of outgoings). Ultimately when you buy commercial, your purchase decision is based on net rent after outgoings (making sure you do your due diligence, which is covered in more detail in chapter 10).

Whereas with residential, everything is worked on a gross yield rather than net yield. This is the fundamental difference to get your head around when you start investing in commercial.

This means in commercial all outgoings are taken out, then the interest repayment is worked out on the whole purchase price — including what it costs to service your deposit. The cash flow you get afterwards is the true return on your investment. You don't need to budget to set that cash flow aside to pay rates or insurance; you just plan on how to spend your cash flow on going on a holiday or (even better) saving up for the next deposit!

See table 3.3 (overleaf) on the same $500 000 purchase price as in the example in table 3.2, assuming you've put down a $100 000 deposit in this scenario as well.

For this comparison, I will use the same interest rate as for residential. (Commercial loan rates are often lower than for residential, which I'll get into later in this chapter.) Commercial rents are a bit higher than residential, around 6 per cent.

For both examples, I have excluded the cost of purchase, which includes stamp duty, legal and so on. They are relatively the same in commercial as in residential. I've kept the scenarios simple so they're easier to understand.

Table 3.3: residential vs commercial property investment numbers

	Residential	Commercial
Purchase price	$500 000	$500 000
Annual rent	$23 400	$30 000
Outgoings	Paid by owner	Paid by tenant
Council fees	$1000 (paid by owner)	$1000 (paid by tenant)
Insurance	$500 (paid by owner)	$500 (paid by tenant)
Water	$1000 (paid by owner)	$1000 (paid by tenant)
Management fees	$1638 (at 7% of the annual rent — paid by owner)	$1030 (at 4.4% of the annual rent — paid by tenant)
Maintenance (plumbers, electricians, etc.)	$500 (paid by owner)	$500 (paid by landlord)
Strata fees	$10 000 (paid by owner)	$10 000 (paid by tenant)
Total outgoings	$14 638 (total outgoings paid by the owner)	$14 030 (total outgoings paid by the tenant and landlord)
Interest on loan	$18 000 ($400 000 at 4.5%)	$18 000 ($400 000 at 4.5%)
Cash flow	−$9238 negative cash flow (annual gross rent less outgoings and interest on loan)	$11 500 positive cash flow (annual rent less interest on loan and maintenance)
Annual return on $100 000 deposit	−9.2%	11.5%

With commercial, you pay the bank and the rest is for you to keep. The excess or positive cash flow is your commercial tenant subsidising your lifestyle, giving you money in your pocket.

You may be surprised to learn that traditionally commercial property interest rates have been about 1 to 2 per cent lower than residential. Interest rates for residential have always been based on economic conditions, fluctuating based on a number of factors but mainly based on inflation. Commercial property rates differ based on risk, and the higher the risk the higher the interest rate. Commercial property loans depend on the property, location and tenant. If you want to buy in a mining town then unless you are buying a property with BHP in there you will need to show you can service the debt if the tenant was to leave. If you decide to buy a property in metro Sydney where it is really easy to find a tenant and the property is in a great location, you could be broke and sleeping on your mother's couch and the bank would still give you the loan at a lower rate (provided you had some sort of deposit or equity) because the property itself is low risk.

CAPITAL GROWTH

When an investor first comes to me and wants to transition from residential to commercial, they are always obsessed with capital growth. This is because as a property investor right from the beginning, we are taught to chase growth rather than cash flow. Buy today, hold for some years, and either sell or use your equity to finance another property.

It is possible that your residential property increases in value from $500 000 to $550 000 within 12 months: a 10 per cent increase in the value of your property. This is fantastic capital growth but the only problem with capital gain is that it is out of your control. Market capital gains are dependent on so many factors. These include (but are not limited to):

- monetary and fiscal policy
- government elections
- infrastructure projects
- migration
- zoning around new hospitals and schools
- airports being built.

On top of those, additional developments around the area may affect rental returns and resale value. So there are a whole host of factors out of your control that can influence whether your residential property will go up this year or not. Relying on market capital gains is like gambling: you hope and pray that your property will go up. And if your property does go up, you're faced with another problem. Equity doesn't pay the bills!

Equity looks great on paper — and we have a lot of paper millionaires in Australia. The problem is that the only way to access your equity is if you can show the bank you can service it. You would literally have to show the bank you've had a 10 to 20 per cent rise in income before they allow you to pull out the $50 000 you made in capital gains. Wage stagnation over the last two years has made it hard for most residential investors to access their equity to buy again. And if, for whatever reason, you've been made redundant or had a reduction in your work income, the only way you can access the equity is to sell your property.

But what about commercial property? Does that have capital growth too? Yes, it does. And it happens in two ways. First, as the rent increases in your property. Second, as the returns in the market drop. These are two separate things, which mean you actually get two lots of capital gains in commercial property. (Refer to chapter 6 for a more detailed explanation.)

In short, residential property will always have higher capital growth opportunities than commercial because residential investment is created for capital growth and you hold it for the long term for capital growth. Compare this to commercial, which supports itself and has some capital growth in the back end. How much capital growth depends on the rental growth per year, plus market growth. As a rule of thumb, for commercial in metro you probably get 5 to 8 per cent growth per year on average, and in regional between 3 and 5 per cent growth.

The interesting thing to remember here is that during a downturn in the market, like the Global Financial Crisis, when the value of assets was going down, investors weren't able to sell their residential properties because there were no buyers. But there were still buyers for commercial because it was driven by cash flow—and, in a downturn, cash flow is king.

The most common mistake made by residential investors is that they sold at the wrong time and didn't fully realise their capital gains. This is often because they can no longer afford to hold on to their property because it's costing them too much out of pocket. So they sell at the wrong time, not maximising their gains after holding it for so long. In commercial, if there is a downturn in the market, you still have your cash flow. So you can afford to hold it until the market recovers, then sell it at the right time to get the gains you need. This is why during the pandemic, when a lot of investors were waiting on distressed stock, only about 1 per cent came on to the market. Most commercial property vendors pulled their listings off the market and held on to them until the market recovered.

Personally, the pandemic cost my family about $500 000 in the first year in lost rents. However, we were able to hold on to our whole portfolio because, even at 50 per cent rent reduction, we were still able to make the mortgage and have a little left over. If you have had time in the market and your rents have grown, you will find your returns have increased. So even with rent reductions, you will still be able to hold on to your property.

As an area gentrifies, with more people moving in, there's more demand on residential properties. But there's also an increased demand for commercial properties too, as more people want to work in the local area instead of travelling. In fact after the pandemic, the rent and prices of commercial went up in suburbs over city properties because of the change in ways of working.

As mentioned previously, with residential, as the value of the property grows, the return drops. But people go for residential because the capital growth at the back end outweighs the return at the front end. If you look at rents in a commercial property, as the rents increase, so does the value of the property. Even in a flat market, when you increase your rent by the consumer price index, which may be only 1.5 or 2 per cent , you're still maintaining the value of your property and guaranteeing some growth. And in a flat market, when you compare capital growth, in residential if the market goes sideways for a few years or drops due to interest rate raises, then your property value will fluctuate. A commercial property will continue to grow in value even in a flat market as long as you have rental increases, so there is an additional layer of security.

COMMERCIAL GIVES YOU CONTROL

When you first start investing into property, most advisers are not going to tell you how important it is to control your portfolio. Most of the time, you invest in one property, then the next. You let the market decide if you've made a good investment. But in hindsight three to five years later, you realise if you've made a mistake or not.

After this chapter, I want you to think about control and how it is fundamental to the success of your portfolio and long-term wealth. If you can influence the direction of your property growth and cash flow, there is a better chance for you to move forward faster.

Commercial property gives you more control over your portfolio than residential. This is because you invest in properties that meet your criteria, for example regarding risk and yield. In commercial if you want a 9 per cent yielding property and you are willing to go to Karatha in WA, which is a bit higher risk, then you will get 9 per cent. If you are happy with 4 per cent and want more security, then you will get a good solid property in Sydney metro. You can control your risk and security in your portfolio, which is important when you build it out for the long term.

In residential you don't get to choose your yield because the cash flow is uncertain. Rather the focus is on the growth instead.

I believe in a holistic approach to investment. Don't invest in one isolated property and hope to build a pathway to financial freedom. You need to look at your big picture. I spend a lot of time with my clients getting their strategy, outlook and criteria right before going out to find them a property. I know that getting the picture clear in their head makes them a better investor for the long term. It also gets them there faster. In order to build out that pathway for my clients, I have to overlay residential and commercial with financial planning plus corporate structures, legal concerns and anything they have currently, to come up with the right strategy.

The reason control is so important is that you want to know with certainty how much cash you will get in your pocket. With commercial you can invest in the area producing the yield/returns you want to get you to your cash flow goals. This way you can blend your portfolio to achieve an average yield or cash flow base. You can calculate with some certainty the type of growth you will get for your portfolio, based on rental increases on your leases. So you'll know how your income will grow over time, and at what stage you can refinance. This will also help you track when you can refinance, and what your ultimate outcome will be if the market growth kicks in. This will help you work out when is a good time to sell a certain commercial property. You can then prepare your property for sale beforehand to get a better price.

In residential you don't get this type of control because your capital growth is based on market growth and not rental growth, as in commercial. You can only hope that certain areas will boom based on the fact they historically have. Whether your rent will go up or not next year will not have a major impact on the growth of your residential property. Growth in residential is also not predictable but market based, which means you go along with the market rather than chart your own way like you can in commercial. You have to wait and see what the market is doing, then make a decision. This means you are more reactive than proactive.

TENANT OR NO TENANT

A fundamental difference for commercial vs residential is the importance of having tenants. In commercial, tenants are paramount to the success and cash flow of your commercial property. Without a tenant, you only have expenses and no cash flow. So it's worth your while not to annoy your commercial tenants. This doesn't mean you let your commercial tenants walk all over you; it just means you need to find a balance, and so it's worthwhile to use a property manager.

A residential property's value is based on the property and location. Whether it has a tenant or not doesn't make a difference to the value of the property. Also if the rent is too high for a residential property, all you have to do is drop the rent by $20 to $50 a week to get a tenant. It's easier to find a tenant in residential than in commercial. In commercial, your property has to fit the tenant's purpose. Your tenant is going to be operating their business out of there, so they want specifics, for example, rear lane access, truck turning bays, foot traffic, grease traps and disability access. The list goes on, and is specific to each property. When we do due diligence for our Unikorn clients, we look for the specifics for each property. So, if your tenant is a café we will check for a grease trap. If your tenant is a warehouse we will check for compliance for the mezzanine floor. It varies for each tenant and property type but we take into account what the property could be in the future and look for it during due diligence to make sure there is versatility in your property to make it more tenantable in the future.

In commercial, a property with a tenant is worth more than a property without. Sometimes the difference can be 30 per cent. This is why the versatility of having multiple tenants is so important. Depending on where you invest, the re-tenancy period can be as short as one month or as long as a few years.

I've had Sydney properties that have taken me two years to tenant, and regional properties that have taken me one month to re-tenant, when the conventional wisdom is that it's normally the opposite. It's very dependent on the location and versatility of the property, and if it is a destination tenant (e.g. medical centres, dentist, hardware stores) or one that is open to multiple tenant types.

For residential that doesn't apply, because the value is in the bricks and mortar and the land itself.

The main thing to remember in choosing your commercial property is risk vs security. For higher yields, there is also higher risk. Lower yields bring more security. If you want something ultra-secure in commercial, then invest in a medical or allied health tenant in metro — but the yield is only 4 per cent. If you want more yield, then you can invest in a hairdressing salon or a bakery, or even a trade tenant in regional and get 6.5 per cent to 7 per cent. But if they vacate, it will likely take you longer to re-tenant.

What you are willing to trade off for risk and security is an individual choice, but it's worth considering before you launch into your first commercial property.

TAKING CARE OF YOUR PROPERTY

The mindset of a commercial tenant is different from a residential one. When something goes wrong for a residential tenant, the landlord needs to fix it, whereas commercial tenants take care of all ongoing maintenance. The landlord takes care of structural issues while the tenant takes care of maintenance. A good example of this is air conditioning: it is the landlord's responsibility to replace the unit when it is broken. It is the tenant's responsibility to service and maintain it while they are tenants in the property. This can apply to things such as cool rooms, commercial kitchens, and so on.

In commercial, your tenant is signing a lease for three, five, seven or even ten years, with a built-in rent review and option period (where the tenant has the right to extend their lease term). Commercial tenants take care of your property because it's their main place of business, where they earn their living, and also most of the time the tenant has fitted out the property themselves. If it's their fitout it's their responsibility to maintain it. They do this because they have clients coming into the premises and they want the property to look in top condition. Imagine you have a restaurant tenant or a trade tenant. Are they going to have a broken toilet or leaking tap, so when their customers come by, they see how run-down the place is? The majority of the time, no. They want their customers to come back and if they want to charge high-end prices they need to make sure their premises are well taken care of. So your commercial tenant takes care of your property as if it is their own, and they will do improvements to it that suit their business. You don't need to worry about anything internal. It's more set and forget than residential.

Some investors worry there is too much maintenance with a commercial property, but look at what you have to maintain in a residential property. If you bought a house, your tenants may stay for a couple of years. But if you bought an apartment in a city or metropolitan area, your tenants might stay a year or so, but they won't necessarily take care of your property. They're more inclined to be in transit. So you might have some maintenance to do — painting, replacing carpets — to make it rentable again.

And no matter what type of residential property you have, there will eventually be maintenance issues that need to be fixed. Heating, cooling, appliances to be replaced, plumbing and electricity issues.

In a commercial property, you need to set some funds aside for the big-ticket items, such as replacing air conditioning or heating, and roof or lift repairs. But it's a one-off: maybe once every five years and then it's done. In residential, all the small items won't break you but they can certainly annoy you, because they all eat into your cash flow. And if you count over a five-year period how much maintenance you put in for your residential property and compare it with commercial, you will find it is about the same. What amazes me is that a residential investor will buy a property and put in an extra $20 000 to refurbish it to get $30 to $50 more rent per week. And they're happy to pay for new carpets and paint. But when they first invest into commercial, they complain about having to pay $10 000 to help the tenant replace an air conditioner and do some handyman work around the property. I think this is because things like air conditioning are a huge capital cost, so it seems big at the time, while with residential it's small stuff that adds up to the same but is not so noticeable because it's gradual. In commercial the tenant won't bother you about the small things, and it's the big ticket items you have to set aside some funds for. The analogy is that residential issues are like mini waves that come along and nag at you constantly but are not a deal breaker. In commercial it's a tsunami when it hits you and you need to be prepared for it. Again this is what we help our Unikorn clients with during the due diligence process.

If you don't take care of your commercial property, you won't be able to charge higher rent when it comes to a rent review — and you won't increase the value of your property. Plus, you will end up annoying your tenant and they may not stay on. It's also worth mentioning that when you own a commercial property, don't be petty about small things. If you are, when it comes to a rent review, your tenant will remember all the things you didn't do for them and they will make it hard for you. There is a balance for everything, so make sure you find that balance.

Have a think over all the things you've had to do for your residential investment, and tally that up. Then in commercial, be prepared to set aside some funds to continuously improve the property so you can get the highest rent possible from your tenants. That will return to you tenfold when it comes to refinancing and growing your portfolio.

Residential tenants have shorter leases and ongoing maintenance demands, which all eat into your profit margin and return on investment. Long-term leases, plus tenants being responsible for most maintenance, can mean a commercial property is 'set and forget'. You send an invoice. The tenant pays you. You pay the bank. What's left over is yours to keep. It's your positive cash flow.

FINAL THOUGHTS

When you start investing in commercial, there are a lot of mindset changes, which is hard for residential investors. This book will help you on this huge learning curve, and I encourage you to invest in further education, because investing in commercial is not a one-time thing if you want to achieve big goals such as early retirement. To learn more it's immensely valuable to get the right mentorship and team around you. You will need a good accountant who understands commercial property, and a really experienced finance broker (don't use a residential broker and get them to do commercial finance — I have seen this too many times and it causes stuff ups and time delays). Work with a strategist or a mentor like myself or one of our team members. Potentially if you want to invest via your super then you will need a good financial planner who understands commercial property (and they are hard to find). Make sure you find a solicitor who knows and can operate in a few states, as you can stick to the same solicitor going forward to make things easier when building out a portfolio.

Items such as depreciation, insurance, tax minimisation and structures we cover off for our Unikorn clients as part of our services — we link them with the right professionals. If you are doing it on your own make sure you find a good insurance broker (for commercial it is best to use a broker than just going to an insurance company) and a depreciation specialist to help you get every dollar out of the commercial property you are investing in.

It's important not to let your preconceptions ruin a deal in commercial, or let your residential mindset create objections to a good deal. You need to educate yourself and learn as you do the deal. Keep an open mind, learn as you go and let the professionals guide you, so your first deal is set up right for your next deal.

CHAPTER 4
COMMERCIAL PROPERTY STRATEGIES

Before you start buying commercial investment properties, it's important to decide on your strategy so that you can be strategic in your decisions, not emotional. It's more common than you might think for investors to fall for a property and buy it based on their feeling, instead of on the facts. This can be a very expensive mistake.

When you're considering buying a commercial property, remove your emotions. Focus on doing your due diligence, and buy that property for the right reason, as part of your investment strategy. It's important to realise that you don't have to emotionally 'like' a property for it to be the right investment for you.

One perfect example of this is a client of mine who wanted a high-yielding property. I found him a petrol station at over 6 per cent yield in fringe Brisbane, but because the petrol station was not a BP or Ampol he didn't want it. His comment to me was that it wasn't really brand name. He wanted to buy the Hungry Jacks in Melbourne metro at less than 4 per cent yield. I know which I would prefer — but then again everyone is different.

Another client of mine fell in love with a property on the Gold Coast because the foyer of the building was all marble and the fit-out was amazing—but she knew that a regional warehouse property was a better buy for her cash flow. It's all about mindset, and we spend a lot of time with our clients to make sure they understand the numbers that will help them grow their portfolio rather than be caught up with bright shiny objects.

Perhaps one day you may buy a property with KFC or Subway as a tenant. But to start with, you have to focus on building a good cash flow foundation.

In this chapter I am going to discuss the strategies you can employ in your commercial property journey — pursuing cash flow, growth or uplift properties — the risk involved with each, which is right for you depending on your circumstances, and how you can build from one to another.

Figure 4.1 is a diagram I show my bootcamp attendees at the beginning, so they can see what the different journeys look like.

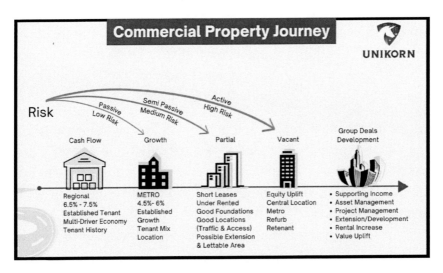

Figure 4.1: different commercial strategies along your commercial property journey

Every person's buying journey in commercial is different. Depending on what you have done in the residential space and how much risk tolerance you have, you can start anywhere on the commercial property journey. I started at the beginning with cash flow and have implemented each and every one of the strategies shown in figure 4.1 along my journey. My clients have followed, and they have all prospered from it. It is a proven journey, but you don't have to follow it. You can choose to just implement one type of strategy over and over again. It is all individual and up to you.

CREATE BIG PICTURE GOALS

When I start a relationship with a client, the first thing is to work through the strategies and find out their big picture goals so we know where they want to end up. It's always a good idea to set yourself some big picture goals for your commercial property journey. Goals keep you focused. They keep you on track. They remind you of what you see yourself achieving. And they give you a yardstick for measuring your progress.

You may choose to set these at the beginning of the year. Or when you buy your first investment property. Or even before you start your commercial property investment journey.

But when you set a big picture goal, make sure you break it into steps, so you know how to get there. (Check out my YouTube video called 'How to set commercial property goals Helen Tarrant' for more tips on this.) If you just have a goal of financial freedom, that doesn't tell you how you'll achieve it.

Have a cash flow goal, even if it is ballpark, then work backwards to find out how much you need to have as a deposit to get you to that passive income figure. Once you know your 'magic' number, you can start moving the pieces in your portfolio to see how and when you can get there. This may require you to sell some of your residential properties, or to refinance your principal home.

However, before you do that, you might want to start with one commercial property first, using whatever funds you have in offset or redraw to test the waters. After a few months, once you see that at the end of the month it gives you more money than it takes out with your tenant paying rent, you'll start to wonder why no-one has told you about this before! NOW you're ready to move your whole portfolio to be more cash flow positive.

START WITH CASH FLOW

The foundation of commercial property investment is cash flow. Cash flow is the start of your commercial property journey: you need to build up a solid base of cash flow before you start on the other strategies. If you are tapped out for servicing your loans, the bank is not going to let you use any more of your residential equity until you can show them more cash flow. By showing them the passive income you are earning from your commercial property, you will be allowed to access more equity to buy more cash flow commercial properties. Until you've built up a good enough foundation to support a growth or uplift property, you should continue to invest for cash flow. You could begin with anything that gives you cash flow—right now, that would be retail or office space. (Two years ago, it would have been a warehouse property, but the market has moved since and now warehouses have a 1 to 3 per cent lower yield than other commercial property types because during the pandemic people started to think warehouses were more secure than any other asset so prices went up steeply.) In order for you to get your yield, you may need to go regional instead of metro. Whatever you buy, you want to get the highest yielding property possible, and right now that is about getting to 7 per cent.

This is not about going to a mining town and buying a property with a 10 per cent yield at the time to get two years of pleasure and ten years of pain when the yield drops. It's about buying a good property with a long-established tenant that's going to give you a sustainable income. Stick to large regional towns, and avoid the temptation of a bit of extra yield in smaller regional towns or mining towns, or you could be putting yourself at unnecessary risk, rather than the worry-free cash flow you should be pursuing.

When you are applying the first strategy, cash flow is the single driving factor. There will be growth, but this is not the first thing to think about. Cash flow will build the foundation for your next property and the rest of your portfolio. Compare yields in different areas, like Bundaberg with Townsville, with Rockhampton, with Cairns, then make a decision about where you will go. If you are risk averse, then stick to metro or fringe areas, and take a lower yield so you can sleep at night. If regional seems too foreign and too high risk, then buy 20 to 40 kilometres outside a metro CBD.

The yield now in the market may seem low compared to two or three years ago. However, the interest rate is also low at the moment in comparison to when I first started investing in commercial in 2012: the yield was 8 per cent in Sydney metro, but the interest rate was at 6 per cent. We still cleared a 2 per cent margin. Today the yield in Sydney is at 4.5 to 5 per cent and the interest rate is around 3 per cent, so essentially you are clearing the same margin, but just paying a higher price for the property.

Do your numbers when you are buying for cash flow. It's about achieving the highest return with minimal risk in your first couple of deals, so you can build up confidence and a good cash flow foundation.

Take a hit on the yield of up to half a per cent if the tenant is a long term or allied health tenant. If the tenant is going to be there for the long term, then over time and rental increases, you will make it up in the back end. No re-tenanting means less out of pocket costs, such as marketing and leasing fees, plus you get compounded rental increases each year, which is part of what makes commercial so enticing.

For more on cash flow, see chapter 5.

LOOK FOR GROWTH

After buying your first few commercial properties, consider whether you would be buying your next one for growth. When you first start out you need to build a cash flow base. This is different for everyone: for some it is to replace their entire income with cash flow first, for others it may be to replace some of their income. Whatever the figure, stick to cash flow until you get close to your figure and then move on to a growth property. This could be an office space or a retail property — one that will give you growth in the long term. Traditionally retail properties have had the ability to give you quick capital growth because as an area gentrifies retail rents are the first to go up and, as a follow-on from rental increases, the value also rises. Prior to the pandemic office spaces in CBD areas have demonstrated consistent growth even though the yield was low. This is because there is so much demand for space from tenants for CBD offices that they keep pushing the rents up. The pandemic has halted this but it will continue in the future after confidence comes back.

Figure 4.2 and table 4.1 (overleaf) show the details of a property that we found for one of our clients from Melbourne. This was his first property with us. It was bought in 2019, a whole floor in Surfers Paradise, tenanted to PKF accountants. It was bought for $2 million and was revalued three years later at $2.7 million. About 35 per cent growth over three years: not bad, considering the pandemic.

Figure 4.2: Level 5, 9 Beach Road, Surfers Paradise QLD—strata property

This property is a classic case of having your cake and eating it too. They bought it at slightly higher than market yield then held it and waited for the market to change and that gave them a 35 per cent increase in value over a three-year period. If you were to repeat this strategy in this current market you'd need to find a 5.5 to 6 per cent yield property in Sydney or Melbourne (most likely an office space or retail), wait for market confidence to come back in 12 to 18 months and you have the same repeatable formula.

Table 4.1: Surfers Paradise strata property

Year purchased	2019
Purchase price	$2.01 million
Area	596 sqm
Original lease	
Tenant	PKF (Gold Coast) Pty Ltd (senior accountancy firm)
Lease term	10 years starting 1 July 2017, including 3% annual fixed increase
Tenant car park	$10 382 + GST
Net rent	$152 000
Positive cash flow	$82 000 (based on 3.5% interest on the whole purchase price)
Yield at time of purchase	7.5%

The yields for growth properties are going to be lower than a cash flow property, but your capital growth will make up for the lost cash flow. These will be in your metro areas, in cities, hubs, established areas, or areas going through gentrification that will have three to five years of growth. The yields are lower for growth properties because they are located in key locations with a good tenant mix, good access to major facilities or roads and have solid tenants. Growth properties are very secure properties as well, so there is lots of demand for this type of property, with the on-flowing effect that the value keeps going up.

For growth properties look for the types of property that will be easy to tenant and will give you long-term growth as the market changes. Your cash flow from here will help you service the property, and go forward to the next step. For more on growth properties, see chapter 6.

PARTIALLY VACANT PROPERTY

Your next property might be partially vacant. It's often a freestanding building, or it could be a mixed tenancy, with shops and offices on the ground level and residential on top with one or two of the shops or offices vacant. These types of property enable you to add value because you buy them under market value. You won't get positive cash flow or growth to start with, so you'll need something to sustain that — likely the positive cash flow from your other commercial properties.

One of the reasons for buying a vacant property is that it gives you massive negative gearing for a short space of time (up to 12 months) while you refurbish the property and look for a tenant. If you're in a high-income job, you might negatively gear a partially vacant property for a couple of years, then build value in it and sell. If you're a passive investor, you could repeat this strategy forever in your portfolio to help you gain above-market returns on cash flow and some growth as well. Because as long as you've got growth and you've got cash flow, you can sustain your portfolio forever.

If you're more active in your portfolio, you do this because it's going to require some hands-on work. If the building is mixed tenancy, with residential on the second floor, it might be possible to convert the residential into offices, which would provide you with further opportunity to generate a higher cash flow. You could keep the property after you have done it up and let it continue to generate cash flow or you could sell it at a higher price point now because you have manufactured a higher cash flow. If you keep it, it will give you higher yield than what you can buy the property for.

You can continue to do this type of project going forward because it's going to give you a chunk of equity so you can go and buy again.

If you're willing to take a bit more risk, this is where you go because this way you'll get a massive amount of money. See chapter 13 for more on improving properties.

Even being busy with all of our clients in Unikorn I still try to do one of these projects every year. I buy either a vacant property or a run-down partially vacant property with a tenant on month to month and then I spend about 12 months to refurbish it, put in a new tenant and then either refinance at the bank or sell it. Right now I am doing a vacant old NAB bank in Gordonvale. I had to remove all the fit-out internally and redo the flooring, lighting and walls. Right now as I write this book we have just started marketing for a new tenant. I am giving it six months to find a tenant although I think it will be more like three months. Once it is fully tenanted I may keep it or sell it. I bought it for $605 000, and have spent $30 000 so far stripping out the property. I will probably need to spend another $20 000 when a new tenant comes in to make sure the premises is perfect for them. The rent when I am finished with it will be around $60 000 net per year and it should be worth around $900 000-plus in value.

If I can do this while I am so busy with clients then you can do this as well. You just have to have a good team of people behind you.

THE GOAL: SELF-SUSTAINING PORTFOLIOS

Your portfolio needs to be self-sustaining. Once you put a deposit on a property in your portfolio, it should sustain itself and continue to grow and support your portfolio and enable you to make more purchases while supporting you. You should not have to support your portfolio. If you constantly need to put in money to support your portfolio because you might be $100 or $200 negative a week, if something happens to you or your business, then everything comes tumbling down.

You could start as a passive investor, move to an active investor, and then take a little bit more risk when you have a more substantial portfolio. It's your life, and your investment journey.

FINAL THOUGHTS

When looking at your commercial property journey it is important to look at the big picture. I always ask my clients:

- Where do you want to be in five or seven years' time?

- What is your retirement timeline?

- How much do you want to retire on?

- Do you need more cash flow or growth in your portfolio?

Ask yourself these questions. Start to map out what you want in the big picture. Then, with the help of your finance broker and accountant, work backwards to how much deposit you need to get you there and what type of commercial property you need for the first deal. If you get overwhelmed by this then reach out to us at Unikorn Commercial Property and one of our strategists will be able to help you with mapping out a plan of action for your commercial property journey.

CHAPTER 5
CASH FLOW IS THE FOUNDATION

When you start investing in property, you are taught to focus on growth rather than cash flow. When you are young and able to work overtime, have no commitments and earn a good income that is growing, there are no issues with investing for growth; you are happy to support your property. However, when you get to the other side of 50 or when your income plateaus and you have kids, a mortgage, and holidays to pay for, you start to feel stretched and your investment properties feel like more of a burden than a pathway to early retirement.

At some point you will stop chasing growth and want more cash flow. This usually happens when the banks are no longer interested in lending you any more money because you can't service another residential property. Plus, you want to find a pathway to retirement and can't see how the pension is going to help you. In comes commercial property!

One commercial property can bring you as much income as one residential property, only with the commercial property you don't have to spend any of that income on outgoings. What this means is that it has the ability to replace your income in half the time of a residential investment, and give you ten times the cash flow. In a typical $500 000 purchase you will expect to get between $10 000 to $15 000 per year in positive cash flow after all expenses and mortgage. In residential you are lucky to get $1000 per year of positive cash flow after all expenses on the same property.

In this chapter, I'll talk about what cash flow properties are and where to find them, I'll show you how to calculate cash flow, explain cap rates, yields and the curious thing called a WALE, and how building a strong cash flow foundation is the first step in achieving financial security and freedom.

WHY DO YOU NEED CASH FLOW?

To have options. That is really it! It's not necessarily because we want to sit on the beach and do nothing. Many of our clients who have achieved their passive income goals in two to three years are still working afterwards. It's because they want to have choices. The choice to fire their boss! The choice to live a better life and have holidays, and the choice to be spending time with their kids.

Ultimately what everyone wants is the freedom of choice. The ability to live life on your own terms and make decisions that are true to yourself and follow your passions. If this is what you want to do, commercial property can help you get there faster than residential investment alone.

WHAT ARE CASH FLOW PROPERTIES?

Cash flow properties are the foundation of your property portfolio. A cash flow property is any property where the rental income of your property pays for the interest repayment on both the deposit, the loan, and all the outgoings, and then gives you money on top of that. I don't mean $100 extra a week, but $500, $1000 or $2000 per week. An example of this would be on a $1 million, 7 per cent yielding property you will clear around $35 000 to $40 000 in positive cash flow after all expenses and mortgage. That's real income you can use towards a holiday, school fees, and so on.

Table 5.1 shows two cash flow properties purchased in 2021.

Table 5.1: two cash flow properties

Location	Property type	Purchase price	Net rent	Annual positive cash flow after mortgage and outgoings	Yield
Chermside, Brisbane, QLD (metro)	Thai restaurant, ground floor retail space	$1 170 000	$72 000	$35 100	6.9%
Hermit Park, Townsville, QLD (regional)	Real estate agent and hearing specialist, ground floor retail/ office	$1 035 000	$77 625	$46 575	7.5%

The difference in cash flow and yield is that one is in regional and one is in metro. Chermside is a well-established suburb in Brisbane. Hermit Park is a well-established suburb in Townsville.

REGIONAL VS METRO

Whether you invest in commercial in regional or metro, it's all about understanding cash flow vs growth and risk vs security. While it is nice to have a property that has everything, in reality you always have to balance one against the other.

CASH FLOW VS GROWTH

If you are chasing pure cash flow and take growth out of the equation, then regional properties — especially in Queensland — generally give you the highest cash flow returns. Growth can be patchy and low, but the cash flow is great. It's enough to replace potentially half your income with just one commercial property.

Regional properties are value for money. If you compare the buying power of $1 million in regional vs metro, you'll see that you get a strata shopfront in metro versus a whole freestanding building in regional. The yield is also 1 to 1.5 per cent higher in regional than it is in metro, so you have more cash flow — around almost $12 000 more. The same interest rate applies in large regional towns as it does in metro, so the upside is that you get more cash in your pocket.

However, the downside is that the capital growth isn't usually as strong as a metro property. But if you already have residential property, that's giving growth. If you don't really need more growth, then you should focus on cash flow.

There is also the time it takes to re-tenant a property should a tenant move out. Typically, it's shorter in metro than it is in regional areas. For example, if it takes you three months to tenant a vacant property in metro, it may take you six months in regional. But holding costs in regional are also lower than in metro so six months of holding costs in regional would be similar to three months' holding cost in a metro property.

There are pros and cons in investing in regional and metro. It's all a balancing act when you invest in commercial property. Wherever the property is, you have to look at the overall ROI on the property, taking into consideration both cash flow and growth.

RISK VS SECURITY

Ultimately the riskier the property, the higher the yield and cash flow return. The lower the yield the lower the risk. For ultimate security, invest in a medical tenant in or near CBD Sydney or Melbourne. Your yield will be around 3 per cent, you may get higher capital growth but very little or even no cash flow — but the tenant will likely be there for decades to come. If you are willing to take high risks, then invest in industrial in a mining town where you can get up to 13 per cent yield, but likely no growth — and if your tenant was to vacate and the local industry dries up, it could take you years to find a new tenant.

Depending on your risk appetite, there are heaps of properties between 3 per cent and 13 per cent yield, which you can invest in to create a balance of cash flow and growth in your portfolio. I strongly believe that you need to diversify your portfolio and that you cannot focus too much on cash flow without balancing it with growth, and vice versa.

For example, if you buy a regional property in Townsville, you should follow that purchase with a property in metro to balance out your risk, cash flow and growth. Going back to table 5.1, ideally you should aim to own both the Chermside and Townsville properties in your portfolio for balance in the long term.

Figure 5.1 is a diagram of the different yields from the lowest to highest risk. The least risk is your ultra metro commercial properties with lots of foot traffic. Your riskiest is your industrial mining properties where it is a destination tenant such as BHP or Toll. They are hard tenants to replace as they don't need a particular location because their clients come to them and seek them out, so they can be out of town or in a hard to find location and it would still work.

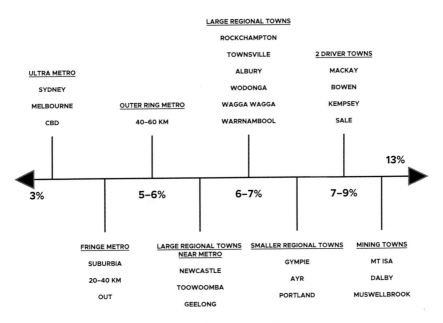

Figure 5.1: lowest to highest risk properties

COMPARING INVESTMENT TYPES

Many of my clients ask me how commercial property investment compares with development projects in residential and investment in shares, or residential property. What I like to do is to simplify commercial property investment into calculable returns so you can compare it against other investment vehicles. In order to do that, you need to look at two metrics: cash on cash return and return on investment (ROI). A cash on cash return looks at a pure return on your cash to see how it compares to a development project in residential. ROI looks at the overall investment, taking into account cash flow and growth.

CASH ON CASH RETURN

Cash on cash return is a simple and very useful financial calculation. It measures the amount of cash flow relative to the amount of cash invested in a property investment, and it's calculated on a pre-tax basis. It only measures the return on the actual cash invested. It provides a more accurate analysis of the investment's performance, based on your cash input, as opposed to taking into account factors such as growth (which can be unpredictable). Cash on cash is the positive cash flow you get from your commercial property, divided by the deposit money you put into the deal. Let's go back to at the two examples from table 5.1, Chermside and Townsville. Assuming the leverage is 65 per cent, the deposit is 35 per cent, and costs are 5 per cent, then the cash on cash figures shown in table 5.2 (overleaf) apply.

You can see there is a big difference on the return on your cash in the Townsville property compared to the Chermside property. You can now compare this to shares, which may be giving you a return of 4 per cent on cash, or residential, which may be giving you 1 per cent on cash. Now you can analyse which is the best investment for your money.

Table 5.2: cash on cash calculations

Property	Purchase price	Deposit + costs (35% plus 5%)	Positive cash flow	Cash on cash
Chermside	$1 170 000	$468 000	$35 100	7.5%
Townsville	$1 035 000	$414 000	$46 575	11.25%

RETURN ON INVESTMENT (ROI)

This is touched on in chapter 3, and again in chapter 6 when we talk about capital growth in commercial property.

For calculating ROI, you need to look at both the cash flow and the growth of the property. In table 5.3 let's compare the Chermside and Townsville properties again, along with other types of investment.

Table 5.3: ROI calculations

Property	Purchase price	Yield (cash flow)	Potential growth (per year)	ROI
Chermside	$1 170 000	6%	6%	12%
Townsville	$1 035 000	7.5%	3%	10.5%
Residential	$1 000 000	1%	8%	9%
Shares	$1 000 000	4%	4%	8%

ROI calculations are indicative because you can never be quite sure how much capital gain there will be in the future. But you can work out a good estimate based on historic growth. You can see that Chermside will have a higher ROI with potential capital growth than Townsville, but Townsville gives better leverage on your money because you are getting more yield (more cash flow return).

Both of these properties outperform residential investment. However, which one you choose depends on which is more important to you at the time of investment. If it's more return on your cash, and you don't care about growth, then go with the

Townsville property. If you want more overall ROI and growth, go with the Chermside property, which will provide lower cash flow but more growth in the future.

CRUNCHING THE NUMBERS ON A POTENTIAL PROPERTY

You need to work out the capitalisation rate, yield and weighted average lease expiry (WALE) in order to work out the cash flow position of a property.

CAPITALISATION RATE

Cap rate is the generalised market yield or cash flow return on a particular type of property, e.g. warehouse properties on the Sunshine Coast. For example, right now, for warehouse industrial properties in Townsville, the cap rate is 6.5 per cent. On the Sunshine Coast warehouse properties are 5 per cent. If you are buying a retail shop in Chermside, you want to know the cap rate for retail shops around the area, which could be 5.5 to 6 per cent right now.

Cap rates are used as benchmarks in the industry so when you are a first-time investor you can see what different cap rates are in different areas for different types of properties, which helps you to decide if you want to buy into that area or that type of commercial property.

Valuers typically look at recent sales to determine what the cap rate is for different types of commercial property. The cap rate tends to change over time, depending on whether it's a seller's market or not. The best example of this was in the Brisbane CBD during COVID. You were able to buy in at an 8 per cent cap rate during those high-risk pandemic months. However, they have now gone back down to 6 per cent or less. So the cap rate fluctuates depending on trends, the economy, and a host of other factors.

YIELD

Yield is different to cap rate because yield is individual to your particular property. For example, the cap rate in Chermside could be 5.5 per cent but the yield on the example property is 6 per cent. Just like in Townsville, the cap rate is at 7 per cent at the moment, but the example property is at 7.5 per cent. If your yield is higher than the cap rate it means you are ahead of the market. If your yield is below the cap rate, then it means you have overpaid for the property. For example, if the cap rate in the market is 6 per cent for office space in Brisbane and you bought your office space in Brisbane for 5.8 per cent yield then you have overpaid for the property. If your yield is at cap rate, it means you are buying at a fair market price. If you bought the same office space in Brisbane for 6.25 per cent then you have paid below market, so you have made a gain straight away.

I always try to get a minimum of a quarter of a percentage higher for my clients on the yield of their commercial property. This way I know they are already slightly ahead of the market and this advantage can compound over time.

WALE

WALE is not referring to the giant sea mammal, although people do like to joke about it.

What it stands for is the weighted average lease expiry. It is an industry term for the average of all your lease terms. So, if you have one tenant with a three-year lease then the WALE is 3. If you have two tenants and one is on a three-year lease and the other one is on a two-year lease, your WALE takes the 3 plus 2 and divides it by 2, which equals 2.5. Banks mostly use this to work out the loan term they want to give you. However, you should know about it as it's a common term in the commercial industry.

HOW TO CALCULATE YOUR CASH FLOW

It's important to know your cash flow figure when you invest in a commercial property. As discussed in chapter 3, commercial property is sold based on the net yield, which is calculated after all outgoings and before mortgage repayments. The reason it doesn't include mortgage repayments is because everyone's interest rate and mortgage repayments are different.

When a commercial property is advertised, they advertise a net rent. This is the rent you use to calculate your purchase price and yield. So, say the Chermside property is 6 per cent yield. The purchase price is $1 170 000. The net rent would have been 6 per cent of the $1 170 000, making it $70 200. From the net rent of $70 200 you now take out your mortgage repayment to arrive at the cash flow. See table 5.4.

You can see you get more cash flow from the Townsville property than the Chermside property.

Table 5.4: calculating cash flow

Property	Price	Yield	Net rent	Interest (3% of the total purchase price)	Positive Cash flow
Chermside	$1 170 000	6%	$70 200	$35 100	$35 100
Townsville	$1 035 000	7.5%	$77 625	$31 050	$46 575

Working out the cash flow on your property helps you to know how much cash you will get in hand after all expenses, including mortgage. Regardless, both properties deliver great cash flow and with one property you have replaced almost half the average Australian wage. Further, if both you and your partner are working, this property could be delivering a third income into your household. It can certainly pay for a couple of nice holidays, or a year of private school fees. This is the power of positive cash flow via commercial property.

CASH FLOW CASE STUDIES

Here are some case studies, including all the calculations I have covered in this chapter, so you can have a clearer picture of how it all works. Please note the cash flow stated in these case studies is the cash flow calculated at the time of their borrowing.

Table 5.5 and figure 5.2 show a ground floor office space with an established professional tenant. The client who purchased this was based in Sydney and was looking for a combination of growth and cash flow so she can keep growing her portfolio. She was willing to invest in properties other than industrial to have a higher return.

Table 5.5: child therapy in Robina

Location	Robina, QLD	Settlement date	January 2022
Tenant	Inspiring Choices for Kids Pty Ltd		
Lease term	3 years		
Net rent	$52 000		
Yield	6.5%		
Purchase price	$800 000		
Capital growth @ 5%	$840 000		
@7.5%	$860 000		
@10%	$880 000		
Interest/mortgage repayment	$15 600	Cash on cash	13%
Positive cash flow after interest	$36 400	ROI (return on investment)	11.5% yield plus 5% growth

Figure 5.2: child therapy in Robina

Ultimately she wanted to have a safety net for her work income so she can reduce her work hours as an architect.

Table 5.6 and figure 5.3 (both overleaf) show service offices run by Asia Pacific, which takes on the head lease over a bigger premises and then leases smaller spaces out to smaller businesses. The client who purchased this was based in Melbourne and was looking for a property with a good yield in a metro area. In South Australia there is no stamp duty so he could stretch his deposit further to get more returns on this money. He was looking to build cash flow to support his residential portfolio and to provide additional security for his new family (he'd just had his first child).

Table 5.7 and figure 5.4 (both overleaf) show a professional office space for a parliamentary member. The tenant is the Commonwealth Government, so it's very secure. The client who purchased this was based in Melbourne and was looking for cash flow in their own state. They wanted a secure investment that is local to them so they can start building a portfolio to accumulate more cash flow so they could retire early.

Table 5.6: service offices in Walkerville

Location	Walkerville, SA	Settlement date	March 2022
Tenant	Asian Pacific Serviced Offices Pty Ltd		
Lease term	5 years remaining on lease plus 3 x 5 year options		
Net rent	$88 895.71		
Yield	6.97%		
Purchase price	$1 275 000		
Capital growth @ 5%	$1 338 750		
@7.5%	$1 370 625		
@10%	$1 402 500		
Interest/ mortgage repayment	$24 862.50	Cash on cash	14.35%
Positive cash flow after interest	$64 033.21	ROI (return on investment)	11.97% yield plus 5% capital growth

Figure 5.3: service offices in Walkerville

Table 5.7: office in Bundoora

Location	Bundoora, VIC	Settlement Date	February 2022
Tenant	The Hon Robin Scott MP, Assistant Treasurer for and on behalf of the State of Victoria		
Lease term	4 years plus 2-year option		
Net rent	$118 608		
Yield	6.50%		
Purchase price	$1 825 000		
Capital growth @ 5%	$1 916 250		
@7.5%	$1 961 875		
@10%	$2 007 500		
Interest/ mortgage repayment	$35 587.50	Cash on cash	13%
Positive cash flow after interest	$83 020.50	ROI (return on investment)	11.5% yield plus 5% capital growth

Figure 5.4: office in Bundoora

Table 5.8 and figure 5.5 shows a mixed tenancy with residential upstairs and a commercial retail shop below. The client who purchased this is based in Sydney and she has a very high-stress corporate job. This is her second property with us and she is looking to get an uplift from this property so she can buy her third one faster to replace her work income. She wants to have a backup because of lot of people burn out in her industry.

Table 5.8: retail in North Albury

Location	North Albury, NSW	Settlement date	May 2022
Tenant	Shop 1 — Salvation Army Family Store Residentials (apartments 1 and 2)		
Lease term	Shop 1 — 5 years		
Net rent	$93 000 (potential at full tenancies)		
Yield	7.75% (when fully leased)		
Purchase price	$1 200 000		
Capital growth @ 5%	$1 260 000		
@7.5%	$1 290 000		
@10%	$1 320 000		
Interest/ mortgage repayment	$23 400	Cash on cash	16.47%
Positive cash flow after interest	$69 600	ROI (return on investment)	12.75% yield plus 5% capital growth

Figure 5.5: retail in Albury

Table 5.9 and figure 5.6 (overleaf) show the details of Oji Fibre Solutions in Bundaberg, Queensland. For this particular investor, it's his third property and he sold the other smaller commercial

Table 5.9: Oji Fibre Solutions in Bundaberg, QLD

Location	Bundaberg, QLD	Settlement Date	2022
Tenant	Oji Fibre Solutions		
Lease term	3 years plus 2-year options		
Net rent	$167 198		
Yield	7.78%		
Purchase price	$2 150 000		
Capital growth @ 5%	$2 257 500		
@7.5%	$2 311 250		
@10%	$2 365 000		
Interest/mortgage repayment	$41 925	**Cash on cash**	16.65%
Positive cash flow after interest	$125 273	**ROI (return on investment)**	12.78% yield plus 5% capital growth

Figure 5.6: Oji Fibre Solutions in Bundaberg

properties so he could buy a bigger commercial property with better cashflow and yield.

SAVING UP FOR A RAINY DAY

You have waited all your life for positive cash flow. Now that you have it in your first commercial property, may I suggest you don't rush out and spend it. Rather, let the positive cash flow accumulate a buffer for you for a rainy day. Work out how much it is for a minimum of three months of mortgage repayments, plus outgoings and some money for marketing and re-tenanting your property, and set that aside. Or, over one to two years, set up a buffer for yourself, so in case you lose a tenant, you are covered. I also like to set some money aside for capital costs, such as replacing air conditioning or roof repairs, and for any miscellaneous items. It is always good to be prepared. By keeping some cash flow aside, you will feel more secure in the long run.

FINAL THOUGHTS

When my clients invest in their first commercial property, I find they are worried that the cash flow is a mirage. They can't quite believe it at first. Then month after month, it just keeps coming in. This is where the addiction begins. They then start to try to work out ways to find the next deposit for the next deal!

The reason this chapter has a lot of formulas and calculations is that you need to know them before doing your first commercial property deal. You need to understand how the cash flow is worked out so you can negotiate with the agents. These concepts may be hard to grasp at first but once you have done it a few times it becomes easier. Following on it's rinse and repeat.

The first deal is always the hardest because you are learning so much as you are doing the deal. My suggestion is to practise on some case studies or some properties you can see in the market even if you are not a buyer. Go over the property deals like you are buying and find out all the ins and outs of it. This will help you to move faster when you are ready to buy.

If you need the numbers or anything in this chapter to be demonstrated more visually then check out my YouTube channel, Commercial Property Roadshow with Helen Tarrant. It has videos on all the calculations and different inspections so it can become more real to you.

CHAPTER 6

WOULD YOU LIKE SOME GROWTH WITH THAT?

The common myth in the general market is that there are no capital gains in commercial property. That is totally wrong. If you look at what has happened to warehouses and industrial properties in the last two years, you'll see there is definitely growth here. During the last two years of COVID, warehouses increased by 30 to 40 per cent in value. Prior to COVID, CBD office space was growing at double-digit rates.

If you look at Chinatown commercial properties in Western countries around the world, they always yield around 1 to 2 per cent, regardless, because they are ethnically based and there is always foot traffic. At one point, Cabramatta (which was a predominantly lower social economic area in the west of Sydney with a mostly Vietnamese migrant demographic) in Sydney was charging a higher rate per square metre than in Pitt Street in Sydney. This is a great example of not letting preconceptions ruin a deal for you.

Growth properties have a different set of characteristics to cash flow properties. There is less number crunching; it's more about historic growth, tenant mixes, and trying to make an educated guess as to whether there will be future growth. However, commercial capital growth is a little different and a little more predictable than residential. This is because there are two lots of capital growth in commercial. You heard it right—there are two lots. And this means that sometimes you have two bites of the cherry.

In this chapter, I am going to give you a quick explanation of how commercial property market growth or capital gains work. There are two different types of capital gain: market and rent. I'll put them in separate sections and then bring them together at the end. Capital gain can be complicated in commercial property, so try not to get bogged down with it. When we do this for a client, we normally demonstrate it on a spreadsheet so they can see what we mean.

I will illustrate it with some examples, so you have a clearer understanding of it.

MARKET CAPITAL GAIN

Market capital gain is the growth you get in both residential and commercial. It is basically looking at the historical growth of the property: seeing where it has been, and using that to make your best guess as to where it will go in the next three to five to ten years. It's what I like to call the hope and pray method. You buy the property in an area that has had historically 5 to 10 per cent growth in the last five years, and hope it will do the same in the next five years. There is no certainty that it will, but you hope and pray that it does so you can use that growth to buy your next property. This is the type of growth I like to have in any of my properties, and you do get some growth in any property, regardless of whether it's regional or metro. It's just that the rate is different.

As a standard practice, in metro, such as Sydney, Melbourne or Brisbane, I normally put growth at between 5 and 8 per cent and, at a stretch, 10 per cent, depending on the area. Remember, growth is not linear; it ebbs and flows. Some years you get double-digit growth, others you get 1 to 2 per cent. You have to look at averages over a five- to ten-year period. A growth property strategy is all about timing in the market. You need time in the market to make sure you capitalise on it.

If the commercial property is regional, I allow for 2 to 5 per cent growth. Again, this is on average, because we have to discount the capital growth in regional in the last two years. During COVID, regional property growth outdid metro growth. We've seen double-digit growth in certain regional towns. I remember I was in Townsville buying industrial in 2019 and we were at 8.5 per cent. Today, in a valuation as of April 2022, the yield has been confirmed to be 6.5 per cent. This means a $1 million warehouse property bought in 2019 is now worth $1.3 million or more.

Market capital growth in commercial creates yield compression: the higher the value of the property, the lower the yield. When the yield goes from 9 per cent to 7 per cent in regional, this is yield compression. Figure 6.1 (overleaf) shows this inverse effect, which also occurs in residential.

The diagram shows that over a 12-month period the rent has stayed the same at $50 000 per annum. An investor buying at the start of the year would have a 10 per cent yield (hypothetical) but as the market goes up over a 12-month period, an investor purchasing it at these higher prices would have a lower and lower yield for the property, accepting a lower return on the front end cash flow in order to hopefully have more capital gains in the back end. So, you can see as the value of the property goes up, the yield goes down. It's an inverse effect.

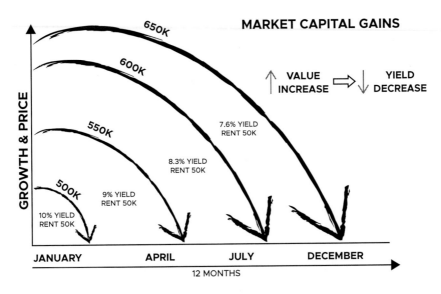

Figure 6.1: as the value increases, the yield decreases

For growth properties, you need 'time' in the market, so the sooner you buy and the longer you hold it, the better the capital growth is because you have allowed the market to gentrify in the area you bought the property in. Just think of it like red wine… the more mature it is the more value it has.

The main reason yield compression happens in commercial is demographic movement and demand. As an area gentrifies more and more people move into the area, and as a flow-on effect more people want local services such as coffee shops, mechanics, dentists, hairdressers, takeaway restaurants, etc. As locals demand more and more services there is only a limited amount of supply for commercial premises, so rents start to go up and investors start to see fewer vacancies. More confidence flows on to higher prices they will pay for the properties in the area.

RENTAL GROWTH LEADS TO CAPITAL GROWTH

The other form of capital gain in commercial is rental growth. In commercial property it is standard to have rental increases per year on the anniversary of the lease. So, if your lease started on 1 July, then every year on 1 July you will get a rental increase ... kind of like a birthday present to you from the tenant. So, if your tenant has signed a multi-year lease, each year the rent may go up by the CPI or a fixed increase of 3 or 4 per cent — whatever increase is set out in the lease.

What this rental increase on your lease means is that you can still get capital gain on your property, even in a flat market. Table 6.1 shows how this might look.

Table 6.1: rental increases in a five-year period

Year	Base rent	Rental increase %	New rent
1	$35 000	3%	$36 050
2	$36 050	3%	$37 131
3	$37 131	3%	$38 245
4	$38 245	3%	$39 392

If you go to revalue your property at the start of the second year of the lease, the valuer will look at the surrounding properties within up to 5 kilometres of your property. (More on how commercial properties are valued later in this chapter.) They'll look at comparable sales and cap rates to see if the market has moved or not. If you bought in at a 7 per cent yield in year 1, and in year 2 if sales are still transacting on the 7 per cent cap rate, it means the market is flat and it hasn't moved. As such, the valuer will value your property at the market cap rate of 7 per cent. The cap rate is essentially the market yield of your property type.

The only difference is that now the valuer is valuing your property based on the increased rental income. You have just had a 3 per cent rental increase, so your new rent is $36 050 rather than the $35 000 you started with.

A 7 per cent cap rate at $36 050 is $515 000. So your property has increased by $15 000 since you purchased it a year ago at $500 000. If you look at the numbers, you will see that $15 000 is exactly 3 per cent of $500 000. So, the easy way you work out how much calculable capital growth you will get from rent on your commercial property is to look at how much your rental increase is in your lease. If it is 4 per cent then you will have a 4 per cent growth. If it is CPI, it could be anywhere from 2 to 5 per cent depending on what the market is doing. What this scenario shows is that even in a flat market, your commercial property will continue to grow, regardless of what the market is doing.

THE TWO FORMS OF GROWTH MAKE AN EXPLOSION!

Here is when things start to get exciting...

Rental growth combined with yield compression (market capital growth) has a multiplier effect.

Let's look at the same scenario again in table 6.2, with a yield compression of 1 per cent over a period of two years, and see how that affects the value of your property.

Table 6.2: property value combining rent and market value

Year	Base rent	Rental increase %	New rent	Yield at purchase	Property value (rent only)	Property value (rent and market)
1	$35 000	3%	$36 050	7%	$500 000	$500 000
2	$36 050	3%	$37 131	6.5%	$515 000	$554 000
3	$37 131	3%	$38 245	6%	$530 442	$618 850
4	$38 245	3%	$39 392	5.5%	$546 357	$695 363

In table 6.2 you can see that even in a flat market the property value would continue to grow. However, if you combined the rental growth with yield compression at half a percentage point per year, you can see how exponential growth is starting to kick off in year three as shown in figure 6.2.

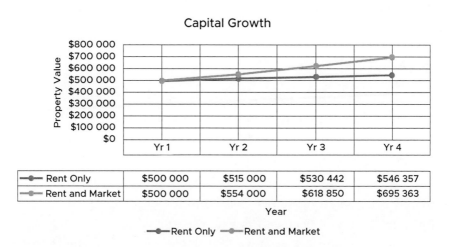

	Yr 1	Yr 2	Yr 3	Yr 4
Rent Only	$500 000	$515 000	$530 442	$546 357
Rent and Market	$500 000	$554 000	$618 850	$695 363

Figure 6.2: rent only vs rent and market capital growth

How do we estimate yield compression? Between June 2021 and March 2022 in areas such as Sunshine Coast, Gold Coast and

Brisbane we have seen a yield compression of half a per cent and in some areas even 1 per cent. So 1 per cent over two years is very conservative. It is always important to estimate growth conservatively, because you can't control market growth; you can only hope and pray it happens.

If you look at table 6.2 and do some research into property prices in the sold section of realcommercial.com.au, you will see that the commonly held belief that there is no capital growth in commercial property is an absolute myth! In fact, if you can get a cash flow positive commercial property that is self-supporting, plus has some growth on the back end, I challenge you to find a better property investment anywhere else.

NORTH SYDNEY PROPERTY: CASH FLOW AND GROWTH

Here is a story illustrating the power of combining yield compression and rental increases.

Capital gains, cash flow and whether a property is a good deal or not can only be viewed in hindsight. While in my time as an investor I have seen many deals and have done many deals, sometimes you don't get to see the full picture of before and after until you have taken a deal from ownership to sale. For this reason I want to tell you the story of my first commercial property deal. It is important to me because it is where I started and took that leap of faith... hopefully this story will illustrate for you the journey of a commercial property from beginning to end. For my first commercial property deal I have tracked for you the cash flow, growth and history of it over the nine years I had it so you can see truly what commercial property can do.

Here's how the selling agent advertised the property at the time.

Shop 4, 83 Mount Street, North Sydney

For Sale:	$425 000
Gross Rent:	From 1/9/12 - $41 057.16
Council Rates:	$483.31 pa
Water Rates:	$882.20 pa
Strata Levy:	$8600.00 pa
Total Outgoings:	$9965.51
Net Rent:	from 1/9/12 - $31 091.65

With the tenant just signing a new 5 year lease until August 2017 this is a fantastic opportunity to purchase this unique property, currently leased to an authentic Japanese dine-in or take-away restaurant. A popular hub with the local business community.

- Fully Air conditioned

- Traditional fitout

- New lease with 5 year option

- 1 minute to North Sydney station

- Set in the heart of mount street mall

- Annual 4% increase

Lease Details: 5 yrs - 1st Sep 2012 - 31st Aug 2017

Option Period: 5 yrs - 1st Sep 2017 - 31st Aug 2022

Figure 6.3 (overleaf) shows the inside view and the floor plan of the property.

As you can see, the property was in a great location and it mainly serviced the local office workers in the surrounding buildings. However, it being my first property, I didn't look for access, windows, car spaces, etc. The property had none of those. It was at the end of an arcade with no windows and funny layout. There was no upside to the property except for its current use. If you

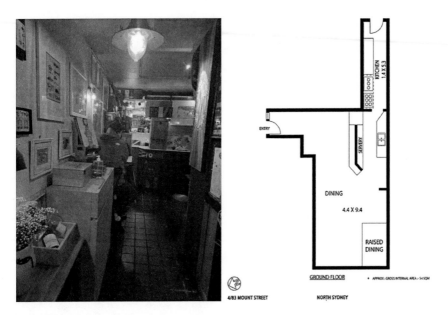

Figure 6.3: the inside fit out and floor plan of the North Sydney property

didn't know it was there you wouldn't be able to find it; it got by on word of mouth advertising. Over the time we owned it brand name tenants came into the arcade and around it, making it a destination hub. We were surrounded by Aldi, Oporto and other recognisable cafés.

The year was 2012. The GFC had just hit residential property two years before and the market was struggling. Investors and home owners were struggling to hold on to their residential properties. Residential investors were selling their commercial investments because they needed to hold on to their family homes. In an economic crisis it is hard to sell a value asset, such as residential property, but easier to sell a cash flow asset, such as commercial property. As such during those years I was seeing property deals that had unprecedented returns I haven't seen repeated since.

I ended up buying the North Sydney property for $360 000. The lease was a gross lease which meant that out of the rent we needed to pay all the outgoings. The gross rent was $41 057.16 and we needed to pay strata, rates, insurance, etc. out of it. Still, with a net rent of $31 091 our net yield was 8.63 per cent. Crazy!

While most commercial properties are done on net yields, not gross, for this property it was done on gross because the tenant was a restaurateur and wanted to know his exact expenses each month to help him budget, so he paid a higher rent that would still cover the outgoings. The lease on the property was a new five-year lease from 1 September 2012 to 31 August 2017 with one five-year option (at the end of the five years the tenant could choose to extend the lease by another five years).

We chose to self-manage this property because it was one tenant, who paid rent on time the entire time we owned the property, and one invoice a month. So we just paid all the bills; it was simple enough and it saved us on management fees.

Figure 6.4 (overleaf) is an excerpt taken out of the lease when I first bought the property.

You can see from the lease schedule that the rental increase per year was 4 per cent. That's 4 per cent on the gross rent.

Table 6.3 (overleaf) shows the cash flow. Growth was hard to predict so I only put the end value when we sold the property. Also, during COVID we provided a lot of relief for the tenant per the government mandate and more. So, the cash flow between 2020 and 2022 was not consistent. When we first bought the property the interest rate was at 6 per cent and we were worried it was going to go up so we fixed it for three years. The interest rate then came down to 4 per cent by the time we unfixed it and then to 3 per cent during COVID. So that was a windfall with the cash flow.

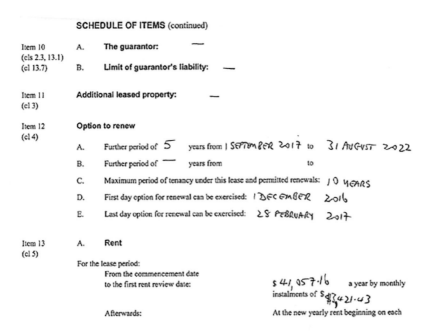

SCHEDULE OF ITEMS (continued)

Item 10 (cls 2.3, 13.1)
A. The guarantor: ⎯

(cl 13.7)
B. Limit of guarantor's liability: ⎯

Item 11 (cl 3)
Additional leased property: ⎯

Item 12 (cl 4)
Option to renew

A. Further period of **5** years from **1 SEPTEMBER 2017** to **31 AUGUST 2022**

B. Further period of ⎯ years from to

C. Maximum period of tenancy under this lease and permitted renewals: **10 YEARS**

D. First day option for renewal can be exercised: **1 DECEMBER 2016**

E. Last day option for renewal can be exercised: **28 FEBRUARY 2017**

Item 13 (cl 5)
A. Rent

For the lease period:
From the commencement date to the first rent review date: **$41,057.16** a year by monthly instalments of **$3,421.43**

Afterwards: At the new yearly rent beginning on each

Figure 6.4: excerpt of lease agreement

Table 6.3: the numbers for the North Sydney property

Year	Base gross rent	Increase	Net rent (approx.)	Interest @ 6%	Cash flow	Property value (yield compression)
2012	$41 075.16	4%	$31 075	21 600	$9475	
2013	$42 718.17	4%	$32 518	21 600	$10 918	
2014	$44 426.90	4%	$34 022	21 600	$12 422	
2015	$46 203.97	4%	$35 555	21 600	$13 995	
2016	$48 052.13	4%	$37 191	14 440 (@ 4%)	$22 751	$619 850 (6%)
2017	$59 400	Market review determined new market rent in the area				
2018	$61 776	4%	$46 776	14 440	$32 336	$779 600 (6%)
2019	$64 247.04	4%	$49 247	14 440	$34 807	$856 469 (5.75%)
2020	$66 816.92	4%	$51 816.92	$10 800 (@ 3%)	$41 016.92	$942125 (5.5%)
2021	$69 489.60	4%	$54 489.60	$10 800 (@ 3%)	$43 689.60	Sold for $1 050 000 (5.18%)

As an area gentrifies the rents go up, as evidenced by the rent review done in 2017. Being a Sydney metro property the yield also compressed from over 8 per cent when we bought it to 5 per cent and heading downwards.

From table 6.3 you can see that there was a major adjustment of rent in 2017 at the option period. This, then combined with yield compression from 2018 onwards, really accelerated the growth of the property.

If you look at the property ROI averaged over nine years, it gave me an average of approximately $19 000 per year in cash flow. Also, in nine years the property price went from $360 000 to $1 050 000 which is roughly triple the price we paid for it. So, on average each year while owning the property and having positive cash flow it also gave us $76 000 in growth, which is roughly around 21 per cent.

So I hope this has busted the myth that there is no capital growth in commercial property.

I'm not giving this example to brag, but to encourage you with an example 'before and after', as all property deals can only be assessed in hindsight.

Can a deal with these kinds of numbers happen again? The short answer is 'yes', but with different metrics. Time, value, interest rate and price point have changed, but there are still diamonds in the rough to be found. Polish them up, tweak them and get the maximum value, yield and price out of them in the long term.

Now it's your turn!

COMMERCIAL PROPERTY VALUATION

The world of commercial property valuation is different to residential. Residential valuations are often more straightforward: they look at historic sales in the area and compare one four-bedroom home with another. Commercial valuations are done one of two ways, depending on whether the property is tenanted. If it's tenanted, they use the cap rate (explained more in chapter 5), which is the market cash return rate on your property, to determine the value of your commercial property. If the property is vacant, the value is calculated on the rate per square metre. If you are looking at a vacant property for uplift, then you will first get a valuation based on rate per square metre to buy the property, then, once you put a tenant in, you'll get another valuation based on the cap rate.

Normally a commercial valuer will only go out to a property once every 12 months, unless you have changed the property. If you are doing an uplift and there is a material change to the property, such as a refurbishment, or you've put in a new tenant, there's a reason for the bank to order another valuation. Banks don't want to re-value a commercial property just because the rent went up by CPI this year. They are more willing to value a property based on a change of circumstances to the tenant or the building itself.

When you hold a growth property, you'd have a re-valuation after you've had a rental increase and some market yield compression.

MARKET RENT REVIEW

A market rent review happens at the option time, when your tenant chooses whether to extend their lease on your commercial property. If you have a property manager, they will automatically do one three to six months before your lease option period comes up. Your tenant has the option to extend the lease by a certain time period (e.g. one, three or five years) as stated in the lease. However, you need to do a market review on the rent so both you and the tenant know they are paying an equitable market rent. Normally your managing agent will get a market comparison of similar properties and rent per square metre. Once the new valuation has been completed, one of four things will happen:

1. *The current rent is higher than market rate.* You may need to reduce the rent slightly through mutual agreement with the tenant.

2. *The current rent is lower than market rate.* You can increase the rent, but if there is a huge difference, like more than 10 per cent, you may need to do it gradually over a period of two or three months, so it does not cause additional hardship for your tenant.

3. *The current rent is appropriate for the market.* You will likely keep the rent the same, with annual increases at either a set rate or at the rate of inflation.

4. *The rent is market rent.* In this case you will most likely incentivise your tenant to take up the option without a rental increase that year, or make a reduction, as a tenanted property can demand a higher sale price. For example, if you have a fixed increase at 3 or 4 per cent, you may only put it up by 1.5 or 2 per cent to make it more appealing for your tenant to take up the option.

A commercial market review is very similar to a residential market review, only it has to be performed before the option period.

FINAL THOUGHTS

Capital growth is a magical thing in commercial property, giving you two bites of the cherry. The main thing to remember about capital growth when looking at ROI on your commercial property is to calculate the cash flow and the rental growth as definite, but add in market capital growth conservatively, as that is blue sky stuff and you can't bank on it.

CHAPTER 7
TYPES OF COMMERCIAL PROPERTY

When my clients first start investing in commercial, they always ask: What is the best type of commercial property to invest in?

Some of them have preconceived ideas, and only want to invest in warehouses or industrial, and avoid office spaces. I also have clients who only invest in retail properties, because they know the rental increase is likely to be highest over time once the market recovers.

Most of the time, when someone talks to you about investing in a commercial property, you think of Westfield or shopping centres, childcare centres, or international fast food brands — all the big brand names. On top of that, you read the news and you think it's a bad time to invest in office space, because more people are working from home. What you don't see is what underlies the industries, and how there are great investments with non–brand name tenants. Everyday Australians, just like you and me, are working hard, paying the rent and realising their dreams of running their own business.

Following the media also means you invest with the crowd, so you're paying top dollar for the type of property that has the most hype.

For example, right now everyone wants industrial, and they're willing to pay high prices. What they don't see or remember is that about ten years ago in Sydney, every second warehouse was vacant and most investors were scared to invest in a warehouse property. Everything comes in waves. You have to remember that it's sometimes better to invest against the crowd than with it, to get ahead of the market. The reason you are reading this book is because you want to invest well and beat the market. If you truly want to de-risk, you should consider diversifying your portfolio across all types of commercial and in states around Australia.

In this chapter, I am going to show you the four types of commercial property that are available in the market, their pros and cons, what might suit you best and what you should expect from each as an investor. Ideally, you should aim to own all different types of commercial property.

Here are the four types of commercial property:

1. office (e.g. professional or government tenants)
2. warehouse (e.g. trade, industrial/manufacturing)
3. retail (e.g. food, allied health or medical tenants, hairdressers and clothing retailers)
4. mixed tenancies (e.g. a blend of retail on the bottom and office on top or behind the retail).

Apart from these four types, there is also resi-commercial. These are what used to be shops with residential at the back or above. Previously, operators would live on site behind their shops. Now you can rent the residential area separately, but you will get the most gain by converting the residential section into a commercial premises. This will have your tenants pay for your outgoings, and also bring 30 per cent or more in additional rent. This is because commercial rents are about demand and supply and generally there are fewer resi-commercial properties about and they have a different feel, allowing for a different layout plan more inviting for potential clients.

Resi-commercial properties have become popular in recent times. A lot of allied health professionals, such as dentists and specialists, physios and chiropractors, seek out residential premises with a commercial zoning, or a resi-commercial property, where they can occupy the whole space. They like the friendly open layout of the residential premises, and feel it is more welcoming to their customers. Recently, resi-commercial properties have gained in popularity, so their price point has gone up as well. It is now more expensive to buy a resi-commercial than a normal commercial premises. It's a lifestyle choice for your tenants, so they may be willing to pay more for a resi-commercial premises over a standard commercial premises. The only downside for resi-commercial premises is often the parking. Residential parking ratios used to be different, so it can be hard to have sufficient car spaces for use. However, if it is in a central location close to transportation hubs, it may not be a deterrent for your tenants.

Now I'll get into each of the four types of commercial property.

OFFICES/COMMERCIAL PREMISES

Strata offices are the easiest form of commercial premises to get started with. They are usually within a strata commercial building amongst other commercial buildings within a business district. Offices are described on a per square metre basis, and when you go to inspect them, they're really just shells. Most commercial offices are carpeted, but some that have just been built do not have any fittings. You'll have to pay for painting and carpeting, and put in partitions (if needed). Strata offices can be a low-risk investment, and therefore their returns are often not as high as other commercial premises. But they are often low maintenance 'set and forget' investments. Unless you're thinking of buying multiple offices within one building, or a whole floor of offices, you will usually only have one tenant.

Office tenants often tend to be more stable once they are established in your premises. I know that there are a lot of naysayers out there since COVID, but if you go to Sydney and Melbourne CBD now, you'll see offices starting to come back. It's only a matter of time before the confidence returns to this sector. In fact, after COVID, suburban office spaces were particularly popular. They rose in value the same as industrial properties, because tenants and owner-occupiers were looking for a more balanced lifestyle, and no longer wanted to travel to the CBD for work.

Offices are low maintenance: it's unlikely that your tenant will have any building issues they can raise with you, unless perhaps if the lifts aren't working properly, and then you'd just report it to strata. This type of property is easy to manage yourself if you want to save management fees.

Office tenants, once settled, may stay for a long time unless they outgrow the premises. This is because the cost of relocating and the interruption to their business can be more expensive than a rent increase. To specialty type tenants such as law firms or psychologists, their rent is often only a small fraction of their income, based on what they charge their clients.

The outgoings for a strata office can be quite high if the property is within a large office complex in a metro CBD. This is due to the multiple lifts and the air conditioning maintenance of the building. Make sure you check to ensure the sinking/maintenance fund is adequate to cover capital expenses, so there are no surprise 'special levies' coming up.

Table 7.1 lists the pros and cons of a strata office.

Table 7.1: strata office pros and cons

Pros	Cons
Easy entry to the market—some office suites can start as low as $150 000	Strata levies—depending on the age of the building and its amenities, the levies can be high (but your tenant may pay all or part of this fee as per their lease agreement)
Low-maintenance set and forget investment	Yields—around 5 per cent or lower in CBD (compared to higher yields in other areas)
Part of a strata—so you don't have to take out building insurance or take care of common area expenses or organise security or cleaning	Special levies for building maintenance may be high—air conditioning refurbishment or roof or external painting of the building or lift repairs can trigger special levies
Easy to value by the bank so the lending process is quicker	Capital gains may not be as high as it is less unique; there maybe over supply in an area which will halt the growth for some time
Easy to determine rent reviews and market rent based on others in the building	Rent needs to stay competitive as there are many comparable properties
If the building is in a good location, then the tenant may be happy to pay a premium to be there	You may need to make the premises more versatile so you can accommodate different types of tenants (e.g. creating the ability for it to be split into two and have two tenants, etc.)

(continued)

Table 7.1: (Continued)

Pros	Cons
Smaller spaces in CBDs may attract a premium because they are scarce—this is because most of the space in a CBD is geared for head offices and large companies, so the space is often 100 square metre–plus; if you have a 50 square metre or 80 square metre space, that may be attractive to smaller firms	

INDUSTRIAL/WAREHOUSING

Industrial property includes storage spaces and warehousing or warehousing that has office and mezzanine floors (a tiered area where there is space for storage or additional office space above the main floor area). Traditionally, this type of property gave the highest return. Industrial properties used to give you 1 to 1.5 per cent higher yields than any other commercial property types, but since COVID, industrial properties now have the lowest yields. In metro, it's around 3 to 4 per cent, and in regional 6 per cent.

Industrial also used to carry the highest risk, with high vacancies and re-tenanting taking up to 12 months. However, with the development of e-commerce, light industrial complexes, with an office at the front of the property, a mezzanine floor to keep stock, and the ground floor to move stock, have become popular. There are often light industrial properties now called small warehouses, or business warehousing, within 25 kilometres of the CBD, which often makes it easier to tenant and re-tenant. This, along with the perception that a warehouse is a safer investment due to the e-commerce movement, has caused warehouse properties to have exponential capital gains in the last two years.

Some industrial warehouses can be split up into smaller individual warehouses, so you can have multiple tenants, therefore reducing your risk of losing a big tenant.

Table 7.2 lists the pros and cons for industrial/warehousing property.

Table 7.2: industrial/warehousing pros and cons

Pros	Cons
Low vacancy currently; in demand from multiple tenant types	Harder to find a tenant for large industrial properties — once vacant, could take a long time to find a new tenant
Easy to manage — if you get a large national tenant, it is a set and forget investment	Property will need capital improvements on it from time to time and upgrade in power
Simple and low strata fees	May have additional maintenance costs
Good investment for regional areas as large companies tend to have large and stable regional offices/hubs. Places like Albury–Wodonga, Wagga Wagga, Orange, Singleton, etc.	Property is functional not beautiful
Good capital gains recently	Mezzanine compliance can cause issues as tenants or sometimes previous vendors tend to build them without council or strata permission.

RETAIL/SHOPFRONT

Retail and shopfront properties include anything that is a ground floor glass-fronted premises. These may be used for any of the following, or more:

- takeaway shop
- restaurant
- café
- clothing store
- medical consulting rooms
- dental clinic
- chemist
- hair and beauty salon
- butcher
- banks and travel agents
- some gyms.

Of all the property types, retail premises are the most versatile in their usage. Although the local council will often require a change of use application, it's relatively easy to convert a dress shop to consulting rooms or even a beauty or hairdressing salon, then to a coffee shop or restaurant. With the uptake of online shopping, a lot of investors have avoided retail shops thinking they may be less secure, but it's the tenant that makes the property secure — not the property. There are secure tenants in all types of commercial property, but retail properties can have a wider array of secure tenants than any other type of property. These include a butcher, a bakery, or dental or allied health tenants.

Retail tenancies have gone through some major changes in recent years. The trusty newsagency and video stores are dying out, and bank branches are diminishing due to internet banking. As such, it's important to find the right tenant for your premises.

The key to retail properties is location. Make sure yours is in a hub and amongst similar businesses, so you can capture the same foot traffic. Check your surroundings. Are you close to a bus stop or train station? And are you near a bank or a chemist, to ensure enough foot traffic? You may find that one side of the street performs better than the other, simply because one side has a public parking lot while the other side doesn't.

Table 7.3 lists the pros and cons of retail property.

Table 7.3: retail pros and cons

Pros	Cons
Easy to convert to other tenancy needs	Usually strata — so potentially high strata fees
If strata, there are fewer additional maintenance costs	More likely to have smaller local tenants over national tenants
Usually amongst other shops in a hub in a central location	Some retail premises are on the ground floor of a residential building and not noticeable from oncoming traffic, so the tenant needs to be a destination tenant; these types of properties don't have foot traffic access so it is harder to increase rents or replace a tenant

(continued)

Table 7.3: (Continued)

Pros	Cons
Rent can increase quickly with excess demand as shopfronts tend to be more unique — this is especially true if it is already fitted out and your tenant does not need to pay any fit-out costs	Sometimes you may have to entice a new tenant by contributing to part of the fit-out costs or paying for removal of the old fit-out
Shorter vacancies — retail can be easily converted to other uses, so it is often easier to find a tenant after one leaves	More likely to have break-ins, damage to property and vandalism
With the right tenant it can be set and forget investment	It may take longer in the beginning to find the right tenant because you need to be more selective with your tenancies to make sure your tenants last in the long term; for example a restaurant or café going broke takes a lot of capital works on your part to repurpose that property again for a new tenant
Good opportunity to buy off the plan and then re-tenant to create an uplift	May stay vacant for a long time if you don't have the foot traffic or if the area hasn't gentrified enough
If an area gentrifies fast then retail rents are the first to go up and they will always be the highest of all commercial rents	

MIXED TENANCIES

Mixed tenancies are typically freehold buildings that have retail shops downstairs, offices upstairs, and a storage room/shed at the back of the building. Alternatively, you may be interested in a commercial building that has a mixture of office and shopfront downstairs and residential units or storage upstairs. Mixed tenancies are almost always freehold buildings, meaning there is no strata and you are the owner of the whole building. Even if the building is zoned commercial, you can still have residential premises upstairs. These types of properties can also be zoned as a mixture of residential and commercial while located in a commercial area or strip.

There are more mixed tenancies in fringe suburban areas and regional areas compared to metro areas. The metro ones tend to be terrace houses that allow for both residential and commercial use.

Table 7.4 lists the pros and cons for mixed tenancy properties.

Table 7.4: mixed tenancies pros and cons

Pros	Cons
Less income loss — since you have a variety of tenants, losing one tenant is only likely to be a small percentage of your overall cash flow	Can be time-consuming to self-manage as there are lots of issues that may come up from different tenants all the time; this type of property is not a passive investment
Easy to find a tenant — smaller tenancies can often be easier to find a tenant for, as they are often small local operations looking for an office or aspiring entrepreneurs wanting to start a shopfront business or a café	Renewals of leases can come up more frequently, requiring more time commitment to negotiate the leases (even with an agent involved) and also more leasing costs

(continued)

Table 7.4: (Continued)

Pros	Cons
Freehold buildings mean no strata fees or strata approvals needed for capital works or changes to the building	More out-of-pocket expenses such as common area cleaning, common area electricity, gardening and general building maintenance
Ability to charge higher prices for smaller rental spaces, maximising your rental return	Smaller tenancy leases may not be as secure as larger tenants; the leases may also be gross leases as the tenants may prefer to pay one lot of rent rather than outgoings on top (most of the time they are willing to pay slightly higher rent that will cover the outgoings)
May have the option to strata the building then sell off each unit/ lot individually for higher capital gain	Potential for bigger capital works costs, so money should be set aside to cover roof and structure costs
Good long-term hold	Need constant attention to balance the tenant mix and grow the asset
Investors are willing to pay more for multi-tenanted free-standing assets, so good future capital growth	Tenants may fight or have issues that need to be resolved

I have now outlined for you the different pros and cons for each property type in commercial. When you first start out, look at the three top criteria that are most important to you (e.g. set and forget, capital growth, location, tenant, yield, property type, strata vs regional, etc.). Don't box yourself in by listing seven to ten criteria — while it's important to have criteria, it's best not to narrow it down so much that you cannot find a property to match. You want to have three criteria that are important to you, then negotiate the other ones you want to the best of your ability, depending on market conditions at the time.

FINAL THOUGHTS

I called my company Unikorn Commercial Property because my clients used to tell me their ideal property is a 10 per cent yielding property in Sydney, with a national tenant, with development potential, under $1 million. That is truly a unicorn. If it did exist, you'd be knocked over in the rush by a thousand other purchasers.

My philosophy has always been to build a unicorn portfolio rather than look for a unicorn property. The person who invests in building their unicorn portfolio will have a portfolio with growth, cash flow and equity uplift, with a chunk of cash to be used for their next deal, before the person looking for a unicorn property has even made their first purchase.

Don't look for the unicorn. Build it!

Start at the beginning and research what commercial property type would best fit your goals.

For more tips on where the market is trending, subscribe to my *Cashed Up with Commercial Property* podcast so you can be kept up to date on what's happening in the commercial market right now!

CHAPTER 8
FINANCE AND STRUCTURE

This chapter is a practical guide on how to structure your commercial property portfolio and the finance options you have. There are different tax implications in each state, so it's important to know what options will work best for you in your commercial property journey.

I am not an accountant and I'm not a financial planner. But I've worked with thousands of clients over the past decade, helping them grow their portfolios under many different circumstances, through refinancing.

BUYING IN AN ENTITY GIVES YOU OPTIONS

Most people, when buying a residential property, buy it in their own name or in joint names with their spouse or partner. In the commercial space, 95 per cent of my clients buy a commercial property through an entity, such as a company or a discretionary trust with a corporate trustee (a company that manages the trust).

Here are some benefits of having an entity when you purchase commercial property:

- You can distribute the income and minimise tax.

- Banks will give you better rates.

- You can have asset protection if you are in a high-risk industry.

TAX MINIMISATION

A discretionary trust gives you a capital gains tax discount after holding the property for 12 months. It also allows you to distribute the income to your spouse, your children or other family members and related entities, to minimise tax. For the purchase and holding of a set and forget property with positive cash flow, a discretionary trust has proven to be the best option.

If you plan to do commercial developments, flips, or to go into a project with a business partner, a company may be the best option, as you can wind up the company once the project finishes.

For different entities, there are also different land tax thresholds in each state, so it makes it worthwhile to use specific entities when you are purchasing in that state. For example, in Queensland at the moment, the land tax threshold is $350 000 per entity, and there is no pooling provision. This means that you can minimise or avoid paying land tax by creating different entities to keep them below the threshold. This provision, like all tax provisions, could change, but it is worthwhile for you to check out the different state thresholds for land tax when buying commercial property. For example, in the ACT, there is land tax on residential property, but not on commercial. Each state varies, and they are prone to change. So depending on which state you buy in, you may choose different entities, or buy in your own name.

BETTER LOAN RATES

The banks also like entities when lending for commercial property because if something happens to the property, or you, and you can no longer afford the mortgage repayments, then the bank can take over that whole entity without touching the rest of your assets. It's cleaner and less messy. They can just go to auction, sell the property and recuperate their costs. For this reason they give a more favourable rate for a commercial property purchase by an entity, as opposed to you buying in your own name.

ASSET PROTECTION

If you're a doctor or a lawyer, you might want to buy commercial property in an entity, with your spouse as the sole director. This way if anyone sues you, the asset is protected because the property is held in a separate entity, with a completely different director. This gives you asset protection, as it is hard to find the relationship between you and the entity if you are not a director of it. Even if you are a director of the corporate trustee that governs a trust, a trust is not registered. So anyone that is suing will find it hard to attack a trust to get hold of the asset.

There are many different options for asset protection. These include having a bucket company — a company set up as a beneficiary to a trust — and also a piggy bank company that creates a loan for the deposit, so there's no equity left in the property for anyone to gain. How far you want to go in terms of your asset protection depends on your category of work, so please consult your accountant or financial planner. We work with some really good ones who can do complex tax structures, so feel free to reach out to us for a referral.

SET UP YOUR ENTITY FIRST

It is important to set up your entity before you buy a commercial property because you don't want to pay double stamp duty. Different states vary in their conveyancing process, but in most states you cannot sign a contract in your own name, and then later decide you want to buy in a different name, without incurring double stamp duty. We advise all our clients to have an entity already set up, or work out the structure in which they want to hold their commercial property before we start looking for a property.

If you are looking to distribute your income to another family member or your spouse then a discretionary family trust with a corporate trustee is the best way to go. If you are looking to do a flip within 12 months, then a company is better. If you don't own property in certain states such as Victoria and you wanted to save on land tax, then holding it in your own name will give you a threshold of $250 000 as oppose to $0 in a trust.

In a hot market, you have to be prepared to move fast, so you won't have two to three days to set up an entity. Sometimes an accountant can take up to a week or two to set up an entity and by then you'll have lost the deal. You want to make sure you can sign a contract tomorrow when you start looking for your commercial property. Being ready to sign and exchange contracts can make you the front runner for a deal, even if you may not be paying top dollar for that deal. In my experience, sometimes the speed of the deal is more important than the price point.

GETTING READY TO BUY COMMERCIAL

You can't get pre-approval when you're looking for commercial property (we'll discuss why later in this chapter). But before you think of buying commercial, you need to speak to a finance broker or the bank to get a general idea of your ability to borrow. I prefer a broker over a bank because their information is more concrete, and when you're ready to go they will be faster than a bank. They also have specialised business development managers within the banks that can help to push a loan through for you. It's important to seek a broker who has considerable experience in working with commercial loans. The one we work with only does commercial finance, so they are a specialist in their field. Each property needs to be properly presented to the bank, and an experienced commercial broker knows how to package up a deal to present to the bank in the right way to get you the best rates and terms.

What we typically do for our clients is to get their profile set up with our broker, and perform an initial assessment so they know how much they can borrow. Then I send some case studies to the broker to run them past the bank so they can okay a scenario. Once that is done, we know exactly what the client can get approved for so we can start hunting down the right commercial property for them.

FINANCING

If they're coming from a residential investment space, our clients often ask us about pre-approval. In commercial there is no pre-approval, because it's property specific. Depending on the property you are going to buy, the bank will assess the asset and give you a LVR (loan to valuation rate) and loan terms. The general rule of thumb is that the higher the risk, the lower the LVR the bank will give you; they'll also ask for a higher deposit, and the interest rate may be higher.

When you first enter the commercial property space, there are lots of shiny objects to distract you, such as childcare centres, petrol stations, shopping centres, medical centres, and so on. We all want to buy those types of commercial assets but they put everyday Australians off, because they think it's too expensive to get into commercial real estate. Large assets, such as childcare centres and petrol stations, are also highly specialist assets. This means the bank will only lend you 50 to 55 per cent LVR, so you need a large deposit to buy these properties.

For most investors, a hairdresser or a physio or the café in the shopping centre is a good entry point into commercial, because they are below $1 million to buy, so the LVR will likely give you better loan terms, and have a good stable client.

RESTRUCTURING YOUR FINANCES FOR COMMERCIAL

When it comes to finance, commercial property behaves very differently from residential. A lot of people think cross-collateralising residential with commercial is a good idea. That is the worst thing you can do in commercial finance, because commercial finance and residential finance don't talk to each other in the banks. They are separate and as a result, it's very hard to try to refinance a commercial property when it's cross-collateralised with residential and vice versa.

The way forward is to refinance your residential property and then get a separate commercial loan, so that the two are not interrelated.

For example if you don't have a deposit but have a residential property that will allow you to refinance and take out $300 000, do the refinancing first. Then once that $300 000 is available you then use that as a deposit to buy a commercial property at $900 000 to $950 000 at 65 per cent LVR. Alternatively you can get access to your equity from your residential property based on the cash flow you'll get from the rent for your commercial property, and also based on the servicing you can have on your current income.

As part of our client onboarding, we do a detailed strategy session. This includes carefully considering the best way to refinance and re-position your current assets so you can have a more effective portfolio. Normally, speaking to a commercial finance specialist is the best way to work out a pathway. Failing that, you can speak to your residential broker to see if you can refinance and get a commercial loan after that.

COMMERCIAL LOANS

The general rule in commercial finance is that if you have a deposit, you will get a loan. It's totally different from residential: I remember my uncle trying to buy his own residential property to live in. He had a deposit of 70 per cent of the purchase price, and wished to borrow 30 per cent. Because he was not working at the time, the bank wouldn't lend him the 30 per cent. He had to borrow from family to be able to complete the sale.

In commercial, if you can come up with a deposit, the bank will always lend you the money. The length of the loan may change, depending on the lease, where the property is located, and the risk profile of the tenant. You may have a loan for two years, or up to five or 20 years. It all depends on the lease and the tenant.

If the property is in metro, with a really good strong lease and a good tenant, you might get a longer loan. You might only have a loan for two years if it's in a remote or regional area where lease terms are shorter, or the tenant is not so secure. However, if you have a deposit, you will get a loan. That's the fundamental difference between commercial and residential.

Most commercial loans will start off with an interest-only period, followed by principal and interest payments, similar to residential loans. My advice to most of my clients is that unless they really want to keep a property, they keep it on an interest-only loan. Every time it's about to change to principal and interest, they refinance it so they can continue to buy more properties and live off the cash flow.

In the long term, the value of your property will go up. You will sell some of them and pay down your debt. But in actual fact, in most cases it's best to *never* pay down your principal if you hold a commercial property portfolio. Most of the time the principal is only paid off when the property is sold when they consolidate in the future.

LOAN TYPES

Here is a quick snapshot of the different types of loans available for commercial property purchase. They are in no particular order, and you'll find out which is best for you when you discuss it with your finance broker or other advisers.

LEASE DOC LOANS

When I say that if you have a deposit, they will give you a loan, this is because most of the time the loan is based on the lease. This is what we call a lease doc loan. Your lending institution will only look at the lease, tenant, location and rental income for servicing the loan, so they do not look at your servicing. This is the best type of loan if you are serviceability tapped out and have a lot of residential properties.

The bank will assess the strength of the lease, the strength of the tenant and the location, and provide you with a loan to valuation ratio (LVR) for your loan. Most of the time, that's 65 per cent, so you need to come up with 35 per cent deposit plus costs. On a $1 million property, you need to come up with a deposit of $350 000, and allow for 5 per cent of the purchase price in costs. These costs include but are not limited to stamp duty, legal and any of the due diligence costs you may incur in purchasing the property. This doesn't include any buyer's agency fees. So to buy a $1 million property, you need a deposit of around $400 000 if you want to go for a lease doc loan.

A lease doc loan does not test you for servicing; it does not look at what other assets you have or how complicated everything else you own is. It's great for a developer, or a highly leveraged residential investor who wants to get into their first commercial property, but is unsure how, because they can no longer service any more debt. The bank normally wants the property to be held in a separate structure to everything else you own, so it's quarantined. Then if something happens to the property or you, and you cannot make mortgage repayments, it's easier for them to take back the property.

Lease doc loans are for the set and forget investor who is looking to finance a pure cash flow property. If you want to buy a property on a short term lease, and you want to do an uplift, a lease doc loan is not for you.

Now you can see why, even if you buy a 5 per cent yielding property in Sydney or the Sydney fringe, for most investors buying a $1 million property, it's still a good deal. They're going to get $25 000 in net positive cash flow after mortgage and all outgoings, without having to be tested for servicing. Without having to go through the rigmarole of examining expenses like you have to do with residential, looking at what you spend on Netflix. All you have to do is show up with a deposit. The bank does the valuation. If the valuation comes in on contract price, the bank takes five to seven working days to approve the loan. Then voila, it's done. You now have a magical positive cash flow coming into your pocket!

LEASE DOC LOANS FOR SPECIALIST ASSETS

For specialist assets, such as childcare facilities, petrol stations, hospitals, or motels, hotels and pubs, the bank reduces the LVR to 50 to 55 per cent because the asset is specialised. If the tenant were to leave, it would cost a lot of money for you to repurpose the asset and to re-tenant it. While the tenant is there, it is a fabulous asset but if they leave, it could take you years and hundreds of thousands of dollars to replace that tenant. This, for the bank, is a double-edged sword, which is why they reduce the LVR to 50 to 55 per cent.

LOW DOC LOANS — 80 PER CENT LVR

Apart from lease doc loans, there is a 80 per cent low doc loan available in commercial for the self employed. It is made for self-employed investors, consultants, or anyone who is working off a BAS (business activity statement) rather than receiving a wage. This is the best LVR for commercial property out there and if you can access it, it's a great way to start buying your first commercial property. The bank will look at your business turnover and look to you to be able to at least partially service the debt while the rent would service the rest. The best way to find out if you qualify is to contact a specialist commercial finance broker. They can look at your BAS and give you an indication of your approval. The loan facility is only one time and up to $1 million, so the maximum you can buy up to is $1.2 million. You will need around $250 000 to buy a $1.2 million property.

Depending on what you are earning on your BAS, and the type of property you're buying, the bank will look at the combination of your servicing ability and the rent on the property to provide you with a loan. The interest rate will probably be a little higher than for a lease doc loan or full doc loan, but the LVR is higher and this means better leverage for your money.

If you can qualify for this type of loan, I suggest that you start there and gradually work down your LVR on each property purchase until you are doing lease doc loans at 65 per cent.

FULL DOC LOAN

A full doc loan in commercial finance is similar to a residential loan. It looks at your circumstances to work out your ability to service the loan. This means that you can buy a property with more risk, such as those with shorter leases, or undervalued properties that have low rents or are partially vacant. If you can service a commercial property loan, it opens the door to many different options for the property you can buy. For most of our full doc clients, we tend to help them get into a more undervalued property, or a property with a shorter lease term. This way they can get ahead of the market.

The interest rate on a full doc loan is also lower than on a low doc loan and slightly lower than a lease doc loan. The LVR is normally 70 to 75 per cent. A full doc loan can take longer to assess than the lease doc loan, so make sure you leave plenty of time to apply.

BOOSTER LOANS FOR VACANT PROPERTIES

What if you are a property developer or you want to do an uplift deal where there is no lease, or the property is vacant and you can't service the debt?

There is a loan called a booster loan, where a non-bank lender such as Liberty will offer you 65 to 70 per cent LVR on a one-year loan term at a higher interest rate. This will usually be double the interest rate on a lease doc loan. Currently, the interest rate is around 6 per cent and it's interest only. The interest is high and it only lasts for one year. The idea is that you go into the property and do the refurbishment, then put a tenant in. Then you transition to a lease doc loan at 65 per cent when you've finished the project. Or you may want to sell the property at the end of the 12 months. This one is an easy loan that does not test you for servicing. And it's fast, because there is minimal paperwork. The valuation is what the loan is based on. Since it's secured against the property, it's a relatively easy and fast loan to approve.

NO DOC LOAN

Remember how I said that in commercial, as long as you have a deposit the bank will give you a loan? If you have a large deposit — about 50 per cent — and the LVR on the loan is 50 per cent, then you can get a no doc loan. It's literally a sign and go loan. It's used as a last resort in case the bank and non-bank lenders have rejected the asset. A 50 per cent deposit pretty much de-risks it for the bank, so they are more comfortable to lend against it with little paperwork. The main thing the bank is looking for is that if they need to sell it urgently they can, and that even as a vacant property it will still retain its value (just in case you default).

SMSF LOANS

We talk more about self-managed super funds (SMSF) in chapter 9, so please refer to that chapter for more information. But here is a quick snapshot of the SMSF loan.

You can leverage up to between 65 and 80 per cent in your SMSF to borrow for a commercial property. The interest rate is usually 1 to 1.5 per cent higher than outside super lending because of the compliance around the loan and your SMSF. The banks have to do more work, so they charge you more. It's also a limited recourse loan, which means the bank can't come after your other assets in your SMSF, or outside of it. As result, it's a higher risk for the bank, so they charge you a higher rate.

A loan for your SMSF and the type of commercial property that will work in SMSF is very particular, so you will definitely need a professional team to make this work for you.

100 PER CENT LOANS FOR MEDICAL PROFESSIONALS

If you are a GP, specialist or in the medical industry, there are a couple of banks that will offer you 100 per cent finance on a commercial property. This means you don't need a deposit to buy a commercial property, but you will need to have money to pay the stamp duty and some legal and valuation costs.

They structure the loan so that 35 per cent is a principal and interest loan to be repaid over a five-year period. The balance of 65 per cent is similar to a lease doc loan on interest only. The interest rate is very competitive, sometimes around 2 per cent for the 35 per cent. The idea is that while you don't have to pay a deposit, you will need to pay down the 35 per cent on the property over a five-year period. This means that your commercial property will not be positive for the first five years because of the principal you have to pay back. However, you save yourself the time it would take to save a deposit, which means you actually benefit from the capital growth of the property while you pay down the principal. It also means that the positive cash flow from your commercial property will actually cover around 50 per cent of your principal repayments as well. So in effect, your commercial property cash flow helps to pay down your principal debt, so what you have to put in each week is minimal.

This loan is only available to a medical professional and is assessed by the bank on an individual basis. Contact us at cashedupcommercial.com.au or helentarrant.com and we can walk you through the process.

If you are a high income earner, and earn above $500 000 per year in personal income (not property income), whether that's from the business you own or your salary as a CEO or CFO of a large corporation, then this loan is available for you, and is a great way to get into a commercial property.

FINAL THOUGHTS

In order to get clarity on the type of property you should buy for your first commercial property, you need to have your finances checked by a finance broker. Some of the loans mentioned in this chapter won't allow you to buy in regional areas, or are based on a certain type of lease or tenant, so it's important to get your finances assessed so you can then work out your buying strategy.

Once they give you some guidelines on your purchase, you can work out a strategy and criteria for your commercial property and the best way to structure your finances. Without knowing how much you can borrow and what type of loan you are applying for, it's hard to work out the right property for you. Finance in commercial is really important to the deal, so make sure your ducks are in a row before moving forward and committing to a commercial deal.

The commercial finance and structuring is individual to you, and what you are planning to achieve. This is something you need to talk to a professional about, so please get the right advice before you start. I have seen too many burn a lot of money because they were set up with the wrong loan or went with a residential broker and ending up not getting the loan.

CHAPTER 9

INVESTING THROUGH YOUR SMSF

One in three of my clients buy a commercial property in their self-managed super fund (SMSF), so they can have control over what and where they invest. They take it as a personal journey to create a better — and hopefully a sooner — retirement through investing in commercial property.

In this chapter, I'll outline for you how to buy property in your SMSF, the pitfalls you may encounter and how to avoid them, the rationale behind it, and why it may be a good idea for you to buy a commercial property in your SMSF today.

WHY OPT FOR A SELF-MANAGED SUPER FUND?

The reason that most people want to buy in their SMSF is to gain control over their financial future, not to leave it in the hands of the fund managers of large industry super funds, who are disconnected and removed from the process. Win or lose, it is not their retirement so they do not feel personal about it.

However, your financial security depends on using the right type of strategy in your SMSF. You don't want to spend 30 to 40 years accumulating super, only to come to retirement age and realise you don't have enough to live on, or that you need to delay your retirement.

When you're in your forties or fifties, you've got kids going through school, you've got a mortgage to pay, you have holidays and all those extracurricular activities for the kids to pay for. That all eats into your ability to accumulate a deposit for property investment. But your employer contributes towards an industry super fund on your behalf. By the time you're in your forties, you would have been in the workforce for at least 15 to 20 years, so there are some forced savings in your super that you can use now to build yourself that nest egg. Done correctly, you can build yourself an earlier retirement in your SMSF.

If you could leverage the money you've accumulated over the last 15 to 20 years of super contributions to invest into a commercial property of your choice, this could set you up for financial freedom sooner than you think. In order to do so, you'll need to set up an SMSF, which I will show you how to do later in this chapter.

Right now, think of having a commercial property in SMSF as growing a tree. With your deposit you plant a seed. Along with water and soil (the bank loan), you can grow that tree, which means you get a commercial property that is giving a healthy cash flow return that can help to pay down your mortgage. While I normally would recommend you only pay interest on your commercial property loans, in an SMSF the bank loans are all principal and interest because the legislation around it is about accumulation — so you need to pay down debt rather than leverage it. With the help of your tenants' rent payments and your contributions to super you should be able to pay down the bulk of your principal within ten years.

Then when you're ready to retire, the tree will be bearing fruit — the cash flow!

The common way of thinking about our retirement has been for our employers to make compulsory superannuation contributions to our super fund while we go about our lives without giving it a thought. We wait until we are ready to retire, then we either take out the lump sum or start drawing a certain percentage of the capital each year.

The problem with this scenario is that we are living longer, and with inflation, it often means that we actually have to cut back in our retirement rather than live the life we deserve. When we start to use our capital from our super balance, we're hacking at the roots of the tree we've been growing for decades.

What this means over time is that the tree will die and you'll have nothing left. Sometimes this will be well-timed. But most often you'll run out of money at a critical time when you need more money for health care, personal service care and emergency funds for incidentals.

Investing via your SMSF in commercial property means that you don't ever touch your capital. Instead, you eat the fruit from your tree, and never have to hack at its roots. This means that in the future, when you pass, you'll have something to leave to your children and potential grandchildren as well.

HOW DO SMSFS PERFORM?

In 1999, following the Wallis Inquiry into the Australian financial system, self-managed super funds were established to allow small businesses and self-employed individuals to establish and manage their own superannuation accounts. According to the Australian

Tax Office there were 593 000 SMSFs holding $733 billion in total assets, with more than 1.1 million SMSF members, as at 30 June 2020. Although this represents less than 5 per cent of Australia's population, they accounted for $822 billion in assets, or about 25 per cent of the $3.3 trillion invested in superannuation.

Over the past 29 years, growth super funds have returned 8.2 per cent per year on average and the CPI has averaged 2.4 per cent per year, giving a real return of 5.8 per cent.

According to the ATO's numbers on the SMSF sector, SMSFs achieved positive returns for the past five years. The estimated return on assets for 2018–19 was 6.8 per cent.

WHY IS AN SMSF BETTER FOR COMMERCIAL PROPERTY THAN RESIDENTIAL?

Before the Global Financial Crisis, conventional wisdom was that you should buy a house or an apartment because your tenant would help you pay down your mortgage. Well, that's not the case anymore! The value of residential property has gone up, but rentals have not kept up. If you own a $1-million or $2-million house or apartment and your tenant is paying you rent, you're so negatively geared that you are subsidising your tenant's lifestyle. The reason that a lot of banks no longer lend on residential property in super is that, while you are able to make contributions to your super, you can sustain the repayments. However, if something happens to you — you are made redundant, or get laid off due to COVID — then the property cannot sustain itself. And this leaves the banks massively exposed.

This is the reason banks love commercial property. Right from the beginning, the bank knows that the property itself can sustain the repayments, so they can approve a loan, knowing with high levels of certainty that they will get their funds back. Commercial property, if bought right, and with the right tenant in place, will pay down not only your interest on the mortgage, but also cover a significant amount (about 70 to 80 per cent) of your principal repayments as well. Essentially, it becomes the ultimate set and forget investment that you're setting aside for your retirement.

HOW EXACTLY DOES IT WORK?

Before I get into the nitty gritty of how to set up your SMSF the right way so you can obtain lending, I want you to ask yourself a question.

If you stayed with your current industry/retail super fund and you have $250 000 invested, could you turn that into $800 000 in the next ten years without making extra contributions?

In my experience, 90 per cent of people will answer 'no'. (If you are one of the rare ones that said 'yes', then you should skip this chapter.)

If you answered 'no', let me show you how it works, step by step:

1. You transfer your industry super balance to an SMSF (explained further later in the chapter).

2. You set up a special entity for borrowing.

3. You use the transferred super balance as deposit for a commercial property.

4. You get a 70 per cent loan-to-value (LVR) commercial loan (you can go higher if you want, but the interest rate will

be higher). Your \$250 000 at 70 per cent LVR will get you a \$714 000 maximum purchase price.

5. Buy a \$700 000 commercial property yielding 6 per cent minimum:

   Loan = \$490 000

   Deposit = \$210 000

   Costs = \$35 000 (covering stamp duty and legal)

   Interest on loan (5 per cent) = \$24 500 (currently the interest rate for SMSF loans is around 4 per cent but I use 5 per cent to work all my calculations to be conservative)

   Net rent = \$42 000 (based on 6 per cent yield on a \$700 000 purchase)

   Surplus = \$42 000 (rent) − \$24 500 (interest) = \$17 500

6. Use surplus to pay down principal because all super loans are principal and interest.

7. Rent goes up each year by 3 per cent approximately, so:

   Year 1: \$42 000

   Year 2: \$43 260

   Year 3: \$44 557.80

   Year 4: \$45 894.53

   Year 5: \$47 271.37

   Year 6: \$48 689.51

   Year 7: \$50 150.20

   Year 8: \$51 654.50

   Year 9: \$53 204.13

   Year 10: \$54 800.26

And so on and so forth. There may be some market adjustments, depending on when you will have a market review of the rent, but as a general rule, this is what your rent will look like each year, as long as you have a tenant in place.

As you get more rent, you can pay down more principal, so you will pay less interest and pay more off the principal.

All property rises in value, whether it's residential or commercial. Since the 1950s, residential property has doubled in value every ten years or so. Assuming that commercial will only grow at half that rate (to be very conservative) that still means that in ten years' time, the property you purchased for $700 000 will be worth $1 050 000.

Over those ten years you have been using the cash flow from the rent to pay down your principal and interest mortgage on your property. By the time you get to year 10, you would have paid off potentially 50 per cent of the loan amount, leaving you with $245 000 as the principal amount owed.

The value of your property is now $1 050 000 and you owe $245 000, so your equity in the property is $805 000. If you sold the property, that would be the balance you have left in cash to retire on, give or take $20 to $30 000 depending on the bank loan discharge and agent's commission. Ideally you don't sell but build up a portfolio of these properties. However, in this scenario you can see how you can turn your $250 000 into $800 000 in ten years without major contributions from yourself. That's tripling your super money in ten years while you get on with raising kids, having holidays, paying bills, and so on. Is that powerful or what?

GETTING STARTED

The rationale behind super is accumulation; when you purchase a property in your SMSF, you cannot use it as equity to buy another property. If your intention is to flip, develop or improve a property and then borrow against the equity, do not structure it within an SMSF. The rationale of SMSFs is that you pay down your debts and accumulate for your retirement.

There is a lot of compliance and complexity in buying in your super. Many financial planners and accountants will tell you that unless you have $200 000 or $250 000 in your industry super, you shouldn't set up an SMSF. That's true in terms of the audit and compliance fees you may pay each year.

But if you have only $150 000 now and don't want to wait until you have more money, there's no reason why you couldn't set up your SMSF and either invest in a smaller property or in development projects, or in syndicates that could see your $150 000 become $250 000 in a few years. Either way, no matter where you are at in your super journey, you should speak to a professional about getting started — or at least start planning to buy a commercial property using an SMSF.

I am not a financial planner. I am not an accountant. So this is just general advice. Furthermore, this advice is based on what my clients are currently doing in their SMSFs. One in three of my clients buys commercial property in their SMSF, and they have a ten- to 14-year plan with an aim to get to $100 000 income when they retire. Right now, based on the current tax rules, if you are over the age of 60, your super income is tax free and so are capital gains. This is why you need to place a balance of cash flow and growth properties in your SMSF.

THE PROCESS

Figure 9.1 is a general flowchart of the process for your purchase in an SMSF.

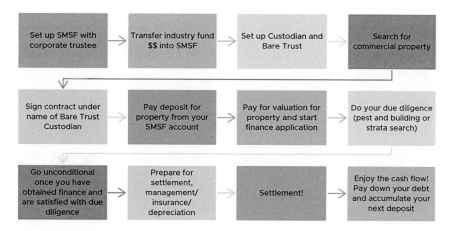

Figure 9.1: SMSF flowchart

When you have enough money in your super fund, and are ready to start investing, first have your SMSF set up by a corporate trustee, which is a company that acts as the trustee for the fund. They can help you transfer your super fund savings into your SMSF.

When you find a property for your SMSF, it is actually purchased by the Custodian of the Bare Trust, who holds the property (and its income). Your SMSF is the beneficiary of that trust. The Bare Trust Custodian is merely the registered holder of the property until the loan is repaid.

Once the loan is paid off, the entity is dissolved and the property goes back to your SMSF. This also means that when you pay the stamp duty on your property for the purchase, it needs to be stamped against your SMSF, so you don't have to pay double stamp duty in the future.

Now it's time to find a commercial property and pay the deposit under the name of your Bare Trust Custodian. It's important to have all of that structure in place before you make an offer on your first commercial property.

BORROWING IN YOUR SMSF

Once the required structures are in place, you need to work out how much you can borrow, based on the deposit you have. The example in table 9.1 is based on a deposit of $250 000.

Table 9.1: how much can you borrow?

Deposit	LVR (loan to valuation ratio)	Purchase price
$250 000	65%	$625 000
$250 000	70%	$714 285
$250 000	75%	$833 000
$250 000	80%	$1 000 000

Table 9.1 calculates the deposit you need, plus 5 per cent costs to cover the stamp duty on the property. However, you should also budget an additional 2 to 3 per cent of the purchase price to cover additional purchasing transactional costs, such as legal, valuation, bank establishment fees, any due diligence reports, and so on.

You've found your property, and are ready to make the loan application. Your contract must have your Custodian and Bare Trust name on it. The bank will charge you for the valuation, establishment fees and legal review. The fees are higher for an SMSF loan and the interest rate is also 1 to 1.5 per cent higher because the risk is higher for the bank because they cannot come after any other asset in the SMSF or outside of super. (More on this later.)

As you go up in your LVR, the higher the interest rate will be. The bank will be looking at your contributions, your deposit, the property and the tenant as well as the longevity of the property to meet its repayments in the future.

For the bank, a loan in an SMSF is a higher risk, so they want to make sure the property is a solid investment. The loan is a non-recourse loan, which means that the bank cannot go after you personally for the debt. Because the property is held by the Custodian and the Bare Trust, it's essentially quarantined away from the other assets in your SMSF. You can accumulate other assets not related to the commercial property, so that even if you default on that property loan for some reason, the bank cannot touch or claim your other assets in your SMSF.

For example, let's say you have $500 000 in your super. You might only want to use $200 000 for the property purchase, using $200 000 for shares and putting $100 000 in a term deposit. If you were to default on your commercial loan for some unforeseen reason, you would only lose the deposit on the property, but not the rest of your assets in super. This doesn't mean the bank won't seek to go after you personally — or your other assets — but because you have quarantined the property in the name of the Custodian and Bare Trust, this makes it very hard for them.

Depending on the property and your circumstances, the bank may ask for directors' guarantees or personal guarantees because of the non-recourse loan in your SMSF. But whether you agree to it or not is up to you to negotiate with the bank.

THE SMSF LOAN APPROVAL AND SETTLEMENT PROCESS

Typically, an SMSF loan will take between four to six weeks to complete, which is about two weeks longer than for properties outside an SMSF. Valuation for SMSF properties can also take longer, as the bank may want to see additional evidence from the valuer. Make sure when you are obtaining loans in an SMSF that you set realistic expectations. Since no vendor will give you a finance period of 60 days, the market being what it is, I usually try to get a 30-day due diligence and finance clause — or make it subject to valuation, if you're buying a property in New South Wales or Victoria.

What I want to achieve within the first 30 days is to get a valuer on site, and for them to start writing the report. Make sure you order your valuations upfront and pay for them as fast as possible if you can, so you can speed up the processes. If you wait for the bank to order them, it could end up delaying you another two to three weeks while your file sits on the pile waiting for someone to assess it. Remember time is always of the essence when buying via your SMSF.

I will also complete the due diligence on the property for my clients during that time. So when it's time to seek an extension, we can be satisfied with due diligence and we can seek an extension because a valuer needs extra time to complete the valuation report.

This doesn't mean the vendor will agree to the extension. But if you can complete your due diligence and the site inspections, and get a valuer out there in the first 30 days, that shows good faith that you are going to complete the transaction. And it puts you in a strong position for an extension — especially if it's only for two additional weeks. It usually won't be worth the vendor's time to put the property back on the market, or to sell it to anyone else.

Normally, settlement for SMSF loans can be anywhere from two to four weeks. At a push, you could probably do it in two weeks, but it's good to leave about three weeks to allow for documents to come out, in case anything goes wrong and they need to be reprinted.

Often when reviewing the documents for an SMSF property, you'll need your lawyers to sign them off, so make sure you leave enough time to seek professional legal advice once you get your loan documents.

You can now see why, if you're buying in your SMSF, you have to play it smart to secure a deal, and plan your timeline wisely because of the time the bank will take to approve your loan.

YOUR SMSF BUYING JOURNEY

Figure 9.2 is a quick snapshot of your SMSF buying journey.

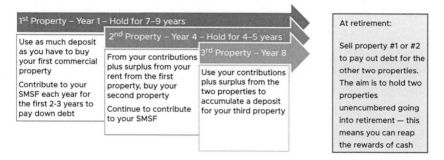

Figure 9.2: your SMSF buying journey

Why a ten-year-plus plan? Superannuation is about accumulation, so the idea is that if you can help that accumulation phase by putting in additional contributions (currently concessional contributions are $25 000 per person per year), then you can accelerate the growth in your SMSF portfolio at least twice as fast. Remember the scenario I talked about earlier in this chapter about turning your $250 000 deposit into $800 000?

If you make the maximum contributions to your super, you could potentially pay off the whole loan by year 10. Then you'd have an unencumbered property valued over $1 million. If this was me, I would sell and then re-leverage that $1 million into a $2.5 million–property and do it again.

Or, if you were to make additional contributions to your SMSF, rather than pay down the debt on the first property faster, you could accumulate a deposit for the next property, which you would plan to buy in around year four or five. The reason for this is that the first three to four years you are paying the most amount of interest on your loan, so you want to have time to knock down the mortgage a bit more before buying your second one. While you're making contributions into your SMSF, you can put that in a term deposit, or put the money into some syndicated deal or development deal that will return the money in one to three years' time so you can be ready to buy again.

When you buy your second property, you will realise that in a short space of time the first property you bought will be able to have some spare cash flow left over from its repayments to help pay down the debt of the second property. When you get to your third property you will have the strength of the first two to support it.

Strength in numbers means if one commercial property is slightly down, you have the other ones to support it. Commercial property — especially in an SMSF — is a long-term proposition. It's not focused on short-term gains.

SAVING A BUFFER

When you start getting positive cash flow in your SMSF, make sure you put a portion of it into a buffer for security. If you need to re-tenant your property, your buffer will mean you can still make your repayments to the bank while you look for a new tenant.

Ideally you should accumulate about a three-month buffer to cover your leasing and marketing fees. If your commercial property is in a regional area, then I'd probably suggest more of a six-month buffer, which you can accumulate over a three- to four-year period from the cash flow your commercial property is producing. Over time, it may be worthwhile to put away a month of rent each year to help you grow that buffer.

This is important. If you are short in your SMSF and cannot make repayments, there are a lot of compliance issues. These could mean that your SMSF is shut down or suspended, and that can be costly to rectify. So, play it safe until the end.

REPAYING LOANS VS GROWTH AND CASH FLOW

Most people think that they want to hold a property that is self-sustaining, and all commercial properties, when done right, give you positive cash flow. However, in an SMSF, it's a little bit different. The bank wants you to pay down your loan through principal and interest repayments.

Typically, they give you anywhere from 15 to 25 years, or maybe even 30 years, depending on your age, for your loan term. So, as much as you love that Sydney metro property, if it yields 4 per cent it's not going to cover your principal repayments. What you need is a commercial property yielding around 6 per cent minimum, preferably 7 per cent. But in the current market, 7 per cent can be very hard to find, unless you go to a riskier regional or rural area.

A 6 per cent yielding property will enable you to cover the 4 per cent interest on the loan, and the bulk of your principal repayments as well. This doesn't mean that you won't need to contribute into your SMSF the first couple of years — it all depends on the length of your loan from the bank, and your repayments.

While you might be tempted to pay down the loan as fast as possible, you really should be looking at a long-term goal of ten to 14 years in your SMSF, and look to buy your next commercial property in year four or five. In order to do that, think about making additional contributions to the maximum threshold each year. Currently that is $25 000, and if there's two of you working, it could mean as much as $50 000 per year going into your SMSF. Over a four-year period, with the rising rent on your existing property, maybe you could manage to contribute the maximum, putting yourself in a position to buy that next property. Either way, it's really important to keep accumulating because ultimately the more you accumulate the better your retirement income will be and the more secure you will feel. You may even possibly retire earlier. Keep your SMSF income stream separate from what you are building outside of SMSF.

A high-yielding property is going to give you more cash flow. Growth properties will give you a leg up into a bigger property in the future, but only if you sell and then use the money from the sale to buy a bigger property — there is no refinance for equity in super. But you might need to make contributions to support it for a bit longer before it's self-sustaining.

If you are in your thirties when you start out in your SMSF, then you want to have more growth properties to begin with. If you're in your forties or fifties, you need more cash flow properties to start with. When you have more cash flow properties, you can accumulate more to buy your second property faster.

Whereas when you're in your thirties, you've got the time to be in the market to let the property grow, and you'll also be able to make more contributions into your SMSF because you may have fewer financial commitments elsewhere. It is counterintuitive to look for a growth property in super, but when you are in your thirties it will be almost another 30 years before you can access any type of cash flow from your super. However, since property has doubled every ten years since the 1950s, it makes sense for you to buy a growth property and let it grow in the background while you are still able to work and contribute to the super. In short, when you have the time to hold a property and you have the ability to contribute to super, buy a growth property. If you don't have the time or have less time, like when you are in your late forties or mid fifties, then you need more cash flow because you need to get to the second property faster.

Super was set up so you started to accumulate when you started work in your twenties, so you have 40 years to grow it while you work. But life isn't always like that — sometimes you change jobs, sometimes you decide to work for yourself (and you don't pay super because it's not mandatory) or you decide to stop work to have a family. For all sorts of reasons you may stop contributing to super. Then you wake up in your late forties or fifties and realise that you'd better hurry up if you want to retire, which is why you need a cash flow property in your super the later you start. I started my parents' SMSF for them when they were 60! So it's never too late to start.

WHAT TYPE OF PROPERTY SHOULD YOU BUY IN YOUR SMSF?

The main thing for any SMSF property is to make sure it satisfies the single acquirable asset rule under the *Superannuation Industry (Supervision) Act* of 1993. This means that the asset needs to be used as only one asset, and is unable to be split up. In effect, what the bank wants in SMSF is one commercial property with one title and on one lot. This is why they love strata properties. With strata, the banks know what it is, and that it's highly unlikely you can make major changes to it.

This doesn't mean they won't take a freestanding property in an SMSF. It just means when the property is freestanding, they need to make sure it is over one title and one lot. If it is not, your accountant needs to issue a letter to say that it is a single acquirable asset, which means that the lot cannot be split up or the property cannot be used separately due to the different lots.

You should not buy a property you want to make substantial changes to under this structure. While you have a loan on your commercial property held under the Bare Trust Custodian for your SMSF, you won't be able to make major modifications or changes to the property because you cannot change the use of the property while it's held under that entity. You cannot develop the property. You can't make improvements, such as changing what started out as a dental surgery to become a childcare centre.

However, you are allowed to perform repairs and maintenance on the commercial property, so you can improve the property as your tenant needs. If your dental tenant wants to expand their practice, you can contribute towards the extension. Or if you have a NDIS tenant who wants a disability ramp and toilet, you can contribute to this.

Once you have paid off the loan on your commercial property and the Bare Trust has dissolved, you can now do anything you want with that property, because it's no longer the bank's concern. So you can develop the land, subdivide it or change the use of the property, even from commercial to residential, or vice versa.

LOOK FOR VALUE AND SECURITY

Ultimately, whatever property you decide to buy in your SMSF, it's all about value. You're not planning to buy a property and sell it tomorrow. So don't get stuck on negotiating every cent out of it. Over time, growth will happen while you pay down the debt. If it's the right property for your SMSF and you end up sacrificing a few basis points or pay a bit more for it, in ten years' time it won't matter, because you'll make that money back ten-fold. Just make sure the property you buy in your SMSF has longevity. Focus on value. Value in the bricks and mortar of the property. Value in the tenancy. And value in the versatility and the location of the property.

If you're going to have a solid ten- or 14-year plan, you want your commercial property to appreciate in value. You want it to be easily tenantable, because, while it's possible you may have a tenant for ten years, the most likely scenario is that you have a tenant anywhere from four to six years, and then you'll need to put a new tenant into your premises.

Security is important in any investment. But it's particularly important in SMSF because while you're busy running your life, you're expecting your SMSF to perform while you sleep. It can only do that if you make the right decisions, and engage the right professionals to help you find properties that suit an SMSF purchase. For SMSF purchases, it's sometimes worthwhile to take a little less in yield. Instead of chasing a 7 per cent yield, you could scale it back to 6.5 per cent and be in a safer location, or go for a 6 per cent yield and be in an even better location, making it easier to re-tenant later on.

PROPERTIES FOR DIFFERENT PRICE POINTS

So what types of properties might you consider for your SMSF?

FOR UNDER $600000

The ideal property for under $600000 is a strata office, retail or warehouse in a metro area, with a tenant on a minimum three-year lease with options, yielding about 6 per cent.

Table 9.2 and figure 9.3 (both overleaf) show some sample properties under $600000 that would be appropriate for an SMSF.

Table 9.2 sample properties under $600 000

Location	Gordonvale, QLD 4865 (*freestanding*)	Slacks Creek, QLD 4127 (*strata*)
Purchase price	$465 000	$570 000
Yield	6.46%	6.67%
Lease terms	Shed 1 — J & L Taxis: 3 year lease Shed 2 — Douglas Auto Electrics: 3 year lease Shed 3 — Jammi Pty Ltd: 3 year lease Sheds 4 and 5 — Gordonvale Tyres: 2 + 1 year lease	Kallibr Homes Pty Ltd: 3 + 3 year lease (Net rent: $38k)

Freestanding

Strata

Figure 9.3 sample freestanding and strata properties under $600 000

FOR $1 MILLION PLUS

If you're buying a property above $1 million, then you have a few more options. You can buy a strata property in metro or a freestanding property in regional. Depending on where you are at in your super buying journey, the decision to go regional or metro carries with it different risks and rewards. If you can, find a commercial property with a five-year lease because the banks like to see long-term accumulation and security, so the longer the lease the more favourable the bank will be on the loan terms.

Table 9.3 and figure 9.4 show some examples of properties around the $1 million mark.

Table 9.3 sample properties around $1 000 000

Location	Torrington, QLD 4350 (*freestanding*)	Walkerville, SA 5081 (*strata*)
Purchase price	$1 000 000	$1 275 000
Net rent	$64 714.86	$88 895.71
Yield	6.47%	6.97%
Lease terms	McClelland Trading: 5 + 5 year lease	Asian Pacific Serviced Offices Pty Ltd: 5 year lease plus 3 x 5 year option

Freestanding

Strata

Figure 9.4 sample freestanding and strata properties around $1 000 000

I sourced a vet clinic for one of my clients for their SMSF. It was a 6.3 per cent yielding property in Wallsend, NSW (Newcastle fringe), bought and settled in mid 2021. The vet has been there for ten years and has a new seven-year lease. The purchase price was approximately $1.2 million. The tenant pays for all the outgoings, so my client simply sits back, relaxes, and lets the cash flow pay down their debts.

ABOVE $2 MILLION

If you're buying a commercial property over $2 million then you can start to look for more yield or a substantial footprint. Once the property is paid off, you can do more to improve it over time to increase the value of your property. Table 9.4 and figure 9.5 show some properties above $2 million.

Table 9.4 sample properties above $2 000 000

Location	Belgian Gardens, QLD 4810 (*freestanding*)	Docklands, VIC 3008 (*strata*)
Purchase price	$4 800 000	$2 200 000
Net rent	$370 389.67	$135 000
Yield	7.72%	6.14%
Lease terms	15 tenancies Retail, medical, commercial tenants	GroClinics: 10 year lease plus 2 x 5 year option

Freestanding

Strata

Figure 9.5 sample freestanding and strata properties above $2 000 000

CASHING OUT

You may be ready for retirement sooner than at 55 or 60 years of age. However, at 60 and beyond is where the tax benefits really kick in. Your capital gains are tax free if you sell your property in your SMSF. And there's no tax on the income you're getting from your SMSF. This means that $100 000 coming out of your SMSF each year will be tax free after you are 60 and older. This is almost the equivalent of you earning $140 000 pre-tax while you were working, before you retired. Isn't that brilliant?

So, what do you do now you are ready to retire?

Sell property #1 or property #2 — whichever has risen the highest in value. Then you can pay off the debts on the other two remaining properties you plan to hold, and hopefully even have a cash buffer left. Hold the other two for a while and live off the cash flow.

Replace any of your growth properties, or any properties that you have in your SMSF that have seen a boom, with cash-generating assets, such as a regional property yielding 7 per cent or above, like the one I listed in figure 9.5. When you retire, it's all about cash, cash and more cash. You need as much of it as you can get your hands on so you can live the retirement of your dreams!

If all of your properties have gone up, sell them all, then use the cash to buy higher-yielding commercial properties, thereby giving you a cash flow boost in your older years. Don't be tempted to live on the cash alone; living on your capital is never a good thing. You're hacking at the tree roots rather than continuing to grow and nurture your tree.

As an example, say you bought a 7 per cent yielding property today in Bundaberg, Queensland, but by the time you retired in 15 years' time, the yield in Bundaberg was at 5.5 per cent (hard to imagine but it could happen). If the yield in Rockhampton was at 7 per cent, you'd be better off selling the property in Bundaberg to buy a property in Rockhampton to give yourself a cash flow boost. On a per-million-dollar basis, it would give you an extra $15 000 in cash flow per year, which is pretty appealing in retirement, right?

Ultimately there are many ways you can cash out of your SMSF commercial properties. You just need to be aware of the timing for the sale of properties (for tax purposes and market trends). Either way, with the right help and mentorship, you will be able to retire much sooner than you realise.

POINTS TO REMEMBER

Here are some important points to remember regarding SMSF property investment:

- Make sure you set up your entity correctly. Your SMSF can't borrow money on its own — it needs a special entity called a Bare Trust. Make sure it's set up correctly so you can borrow to buy your commercial property.

- The SMSF receives rental income and pays for all operating expenses and loan repayments.

- You can only hold one property per structure, so every time you want to buy a property with bank finance you need to set up a new entity.

- Once the loan is paid out the property will be owned directly by the SMSF.

- Work with a professional to design a future outcome and get the right structure before you start.

- Understand that SMSF is for accumulation, and that you need to have patience and stick to a plan.

- Start ASAP! You never make up for lost cash flow or capital gains if you wait.

- Invest in some education so you know what you are investing in.

- Find a mentor or a community and have someone that you can troubleshoot with because the journey is long, and you will have questions and issues.

Good luck and start now!

— FINAL THOUGHTS —

No matter where you are starting out on your SMSF journey, there will always be a right commercial property for you. It may take you a while to find, but you will find it. Once you do, it will totally change your destiny and retirement. It's a very exciting journey. I love seeing the results for my clients two to three years down the track, then seeing them buy their next property in their SMSF in four to five years' time, in the journey I laid out for them.

I think as investors, we all want a pathway to get us to financial freedom. Most of us want it yesterday (me especially), but you need to understand that SMSF investments take time. They take care. They take advice from professionals who really understand this space, and what is the right criteria for the pathway you are trying to create for your retirement. Every one of us is different: a doctor will want a different mix in their SMSF than a beauty therapist.

Whatever your situation, you owe it to yourself to explore this strategy and give yourself a chance to set yourself up for life.

CHAPTER 10
PUTTING THE DEAL TOGETHER

The commercial property buying process can be daunting. Most of the time, depending on which state in Australia you buy in, the contracts are different, the legal process is different and timing for your offer varies. On top of that, the conditions in the offer can vary from state to state. You don't want to get it wrong because you will lose credibility, which may affect the deal. In this chapter, I am going to take you through the purchasing process, focusing primarily on New South Wales, Victoria and Queensland (the rest of the states vary and are hybrids of those three states), then go into detail on due diligence and negotiating your deal. But first I'll give you a quick insight into my offer process.

MY OFFER PROCESS

Normally I don't even spend time going through the lease from beginning to end, word by word, until an offer has been accepted. I read the basics of the lease: the tenancy schedule (which covers who pays the outgoings, the base rent, and the rental increases), the definitions around outgoings, any lease break clauses, and any particular rental incentives or abatements that may have been negotiated with the tenant. By then I've got a broad understanding of the tenant and what they do. I may do an internet search on the tenant and look at their business, the surrounding tenancies, the area, and any upcoming infrastructure work. Then I'm ready to make an offer on the property.

If you're thinking maybe that because I look at properties every day it's easier for me to assess, I don't believe that's true. It's because I know that in this market — or in any market — if you want to grab a deal, you need to move fast, especially if you're up against professional investors. Plus, now you have this book, you have the foundational knowledge you need to get started.

MAKING AN OFFER

In residential we are taught to get all our ducks in a row before making an offer. If this is your approach in commercial, you're going to miss out on a lot of deals. You need to learn to make an offer knowing only 20 per cent of the information on the property, as for most commercial property deals you can only do full due diligence after you exchange contracts.

You might be assessing ten or 20 properties. You can shortlist a few, then, perhaps after reviewing the lease and information memorandum, you might have narrowed it down to two properties that you think will suit your criteria. Rather than try to do more due diligence, you need to now make an offer to see if the vendor will match your expectations in price and terms. You don't want to be lining up all your ducks, only to find that someone else has made an offer. In Sydney and Melbourne you normally do your due diligence prior to exchange of contract, but generally we don't like that as it's a rush — we actually prefer to do due diligence while under contract so we know we have time to go through everything rather than rush and worry about being gazumped.

I always try to make an offer just low enough for them to consider, but not so low or with so many conditions that they immediately reject it. Whether you have room for negotiation depends on where your property is located and where the market is. As I am writing this book, we're in a seller's market. This means there are ten purchasers for every one property, so you don't have much room to negotiate. In a flat market or a buyer's market, you will have more opportunities to negotiate.

Some vendors are firm on their price point. Some want an unconditional contract, but price is not an issue. Some are happy to just sell off the assets, while other vendors have a timeline they need to adhere to. Whether these priorities align with yours will only become evident when you make an offer. So the faster you make an offer, the less time and resources you waste on deals that are not going to work.

Without making offers, you will never know if you can secure a deal. However, don't be a smartie and make ten offers on ten properties, because that's only going to get you into strife. Make conscious, well thought out offers.

For a template on how to make offers or to watch a short video about it, go to cashedupcommercial.com.au.

QUEENSLAND CONTRACT AND PROCESS

Queensland is the most liberal state, with due diligence and finance clauses available in most contracts. The due diligence and finance period is normally 14 to 30 days, depending on the property price point, how long the property has been on the market, and how secure the tenant is. The shorter and cleaner the terms, the more likely the offer will be accepted.

When buying in Queensland, there are little to no disclosures. Everything is up to you to enquire and find out. What you don't ask, you don't get and it's really buyer beware. So it is really important to make sure you set aside enough time for due diligence. Missing something could cost you thousands of dollars in the future. This is why you need 14, 21 or 30 days for due diligence and finance. Depending on the property, it can take two weeks just to do a council search, or to get an engineer or roofer. Even pest and building inspections in Queensland can have a waitlist and may need to be booked two to three weeks in advance.

In Queensland, a contract is only 22 pages. It's a standard Real Estate Institute contract, and most of the time the agents draw up the contract rather than solicitors. This means that you are expected to sign a contract the moment the offer is accepted, and, since you have a due diligence and finance period that allows you to do all the searches you want on the property, there's no reason why you can't sign the contract within 24 hours. Remember in Queensland that time is of the essence. If you don't sign the contract, the property is not yours, so it's in your best interest to sign the contract as soon as possible.

If you're buying in Queensland I suggest your due diligence include a pest and building inspection or a strata search, plus additional information about the tenants, capital works, and zoning approvals on the property, as well as conditioning and fire compliance.

VICTORIA CONTRACT AND PROCESS

In Victoria, it's unlikely that you will get a due diligence clause, but you can always ask for it. Most of the time they will give you a finance clause. Sometimes, if you're buying in Melbourne, the vendor may be reluctant to give you a finance period, but they may allow for a valuation clause and a strata search clause (if you're lucky). The reason for not giving you a due diligence and finance term is that in Melbourne contracts the disclosure is very extensive. They disclose almost all of the historic approvals of the property in the contract, so therefore you don't have to do as many additional searches. The time it takes to draw up the contract is usually long enough for you to secure financing and due diligence before it's ready.

In Victoria, the contract is about 300 pages, and they disclose everything. It will take some time for your solicitor to review it and seek any additional information before the contract is signed and exchanged. The standard deposit in Victoria is 10 per cent. You can seek a 5 per cent deposit, but it may not be accepted.

Due to the length of the contract, the vendor usually allows anywhere from three to five days for you to sign and exchange, so this could buy you time to do your due diligence. It can also take the vendor's solicitor two to three weeks to get a contract drawn up. So again, this will give you time to do the due diligence and finance before the contract is ready.

When you do your due diligence, the most common issue I've found is information memorandums not matching the lease or contract. One property in East Melbourne was supposed to have two car spaces paying a net rent of $35 000, but upon inspection turned out to have no car parking at all. The building itself did not have a single car space! The tenant turned out to be paying gross rent, meaning the purchase price should have been significantly lower than what was quoted. Apparently no-one in the office verified this before putting it online and to market. So make sure you verify the information the agents have told you before you enter into the contract or during the due diligence period while under contract.

Settlement in Victoria is generally longer than in any other state with 30, 60 or 90 days' allowance. Normally, vendors prefer to exchange contracts unconditionally and have a longer settlement. So, if you need to secure a property and have reasonable assurance you will get finance, you can secure it under an unconditional 90-day settlement contract.

Regional Victoria is more investor friendly, allowing for a due diligence and finance period, compared to Melbourne metro.

If you are buying in Melbourne and Victoria, make sure you do your due diligence as fast as possible before the contract is issued. The clock on your deal starts to run down from the moment your offer is accepted.

NEW SOUTH WALES CONTRACT AND PROCESS

In New South Wales, especially in Sydney, there are no clauses for due diligence or finance. Everything is done up front, and you have to exchange a contract unconditionally for settlement within six weeks. Unfortunately that's not very friendly for a first-time purchaser. A first-time purchaser will struggle to do all of the due diligence and get their finance done before they exchange contracts, and in the end, they might get gazumped. In New South Wales you have the highest probability of being gazumped, so you have to move fast.

If we're looking at a deal in New South Wales for our clients, typically, we turn that deal around within 12 to 48 hours so the client can be ready to exchange contracts within the week. We're not going to get a valuer out there within the week, but we can certainly do our due diligence, inspect the property, request all the documents, and assess all the documents within that time. Most of the time if people are selling metro properties, they have a due diligence pack ready to go, so most of that information is there.

In New South Wales, a contract is about 160 to 180 pages long. It will have the disclosure statements for the property in its current condition—but it won't give you historic approvals on the site like you get in Victoria. However, it will give you your strata approvals and any by-laws. It will give you all the essential information you need to assess the property now. You'll probably need to still do a strata search or a pest and building inspection on top of what's disclosed in the contract. So there is additional due diligence work you need to do on top of what is disclosed in the contract. It is more work than Melbourne contracts and less work than Queensland contracts.

If it's in regional New South Wales, valuers can typically take three to four weeks. But if it's in metro, it can be as fast as three to five days. In New South Wales the expectation is that once you have an offer that's been accepted, a sales advice is issued — this means the offer is accepted, however be aware this is not binding until you have actually exchanged contracts. Even though you put a deposit forward, your sales advice is not binding until you exchange a contract. So you're still on a timeline and a deadline until you do.

OTHER STATES AND ADDITIONAL RESOURCES

Depending on which state you buy in, we have specialists in that area and we run through it for you when you start the purchase. If you want additional information on buying in different states go to cashedupcommercial.com.au where there is a section on due diligence covering the different states.

Also, when I go into a new state and I am unsure how it works I normally find a local solicitor or ask for a referral from my current solicitor. I pay for the solicitor's time to walk me through the contracts and local conveyance practices and ask for any tips they have on buying in the state. For example, when we first went into Adelaide we engaged a local solicitor who ran us through the process of purchasing a commercial property in South Australia and his advice to me was don't buy outside Adelaide — it is very hard to sell if you buy outside of Adelaide. This is a good tip for new investors, and I've never looked past about 30 to 40 kilometres outside of Adelaide. So I've ruled out smaller regional towns for our clients (unless they specifically ask for it) in South Australia because in the long term we want the commercial property we recommend to be liquid in case our clients need to liquidate for an emergency.

DUE DILIGENCE

Commercial property purchasing isn't like residential, where you see a house, walk through it in an inspection and what you see is what you get. You get a pest and building report, and then make an offer. But in a commercial property transaction, what you see in a property inspection — or in an information memorandum or even on a lease — is just 20 per cent of the deal. It's just the tip of the iceberg.

You really need to do your due diligence to find the other 80 per cent. The rest of the 80 per cent includes your valuation and finance, plus due diligence specific to your property type, tenant, location and lease. As already discussed, in different states this due diligence period varies on whether you can do it before or after you exchange contracts.

Due diligence is paramount in commercial property. But it's very much buyer beware, because if you don't ask you don't get. What I'm about to show you in this chapter only scratches the surface. Having a good team of professionals around you (buyer's agents, solicitors) will help with due diligence. Each due diligence process varies slightly, due to the tenant and the property, along with the age of the property and the property type, so if your team is experienced they will know what is specific to that industry and the tenant type, so they can look deeper.

No matter which state you buy in, it's always worthwhile to find out the process when you start your commercial purchase, so you know how to buy in the right way. Remember a real estate agent works for the vendor, not for you. So it's best if you seek a professional buyer's agent or a local solicitor to take you through the process.

The due diligence process depends on the property you're buying, such as a warehouse, or retail, or office space, because they have different aspects that we're looking for. Then on top of that is the tenant and what's specific to them, such as grease traps, specialist plumbing (for a dentist), three-phase power and mezzanine floors for industrial properties, etc. Knowing what is specific for each tenant comes from experience doing deals.

One particular deal I did a few years back on a property in Ipswich in the Brisbane fringe had an encroachment that neither solicitor could work out. It was going back and forth between the solicitors and the bank and holding up the deal. The solicitors thought they needed to list the encroachment under the title section of the contract, so the bank was looking for a separate property. It finally came back to me to look at what was wrong. As soon as I saw it I knew the encroachment was the balcony on the second floor that overhangs onto crown land, so there was a registered encroachment and each year a nominal land lease bill had to be paid.

I was able to show them that it wasn't a different property but an encroachment, because I'd had the same issue on a Rockhampton funeral parlour property a couple of years before. I showed the bank and the solicitor the Rockhampton notice and explained the matter. This cleared everything up and we were able to proceed with the deal.

We usually pick up a lot during the inspection of a property and we look for things that are specific to the tenant, as mentioned before. Someone from our team inspects any property a client is buying so we can pick up any areas that may have been glossed over.

There are three parts to due diligence, relating to the:

1. tenant

2. compliance

3. property.

TENANT DUE DILIGENCE

Tenant due diligence is all about the tenant, specifically their industry. Be aware that sometimes there is sensitive information the tenants do not want you to see, such as permits (e.g. licence to trade), or if you have a government tenant it can be hard to get access because of the red tape. Check the tenant ledgers, tenant history and the tenant's business operations. Remember, one of your biggest assets in commercial is your tenant, so think of your tenant as your long-term asset rather than as dispensable. Because we go through hundreds of property deals each year, we've seen every different type of tenant and what's specific to them and their industry. So we blend our standard due diligence questions with specific industry knowledge on the tenant.

For example, if you have a tenant who is a baker, questions we would ask would include:

- Who owns the equipment?

- Who services the equipment?

- Do they have seamless floors, to avoid OH&S issues?

- Do they need a grease trap?

- What type of cooling system do they have?

- Do they have relevant insurances in place?

- How long have they been there?

- What is their trading history?

If you have a restaurant tenant, then our questions would include:

- Who did the commercial kitchen fit-out?

- Is there seamless flooring?

- Do they have a fryer?

- Do they have a licensed outdoor area, or are they just putting stuff outside without council approval?

- Are there any trip hazards in the property?

- Does it have sprinkler systems?

- Is there disability access or disability toilets?

These can all affect insurance and have an impact on the business as well.

If you're looking at a trade tenant, for example in a warehouse, our questions would include:

- What specialist equipment that they own is attached to the property?

- Will it be removed, and will that affect your valuation and bank lending?

- Are there any runoffs? (E.g. if they're a diesel mechanic, any runoffs could be land contamination.)

- How are they actually removing their oils, how are they filtering them, and how are they dealing with waste?

- If they have any pits, are they going to be filled?

- Would we have higher insurance due to the nature of their business? (E.g. tyre shops are prone to fires and have higher insurance rates.)

- Who will pay for a higher excess if the business is subject to that?

If you have an office tenant our questions would include:

- If the office tenant has done their own layout, has that had strata approval, or have they just done it themselves?

- Have they changed anything, such as taken down a dividing wall that will need to go back up when they leave?

- Do they have access to parking?

- Where are their clients going to park?

- Who's responsible for the flooring, the kitchenette, the blinds? Do you need to get insurance for those?

- If you are taking a bigger premises in an office building and making it into smaller premises, is it going to be hard to get strata approval?

- Is it going to be difficult for dual tenancy?

- What are the trading hours?

- Can your tenants access the building after hours?

- Are there amenities for the tenant, such as showers or a gym?

There are different aspects that are specific to different tenants. For example, a typical fit-out for a dentist is between $400 000 and $500 000. We need to see their plumbing to make sure that it's all plumbed in correctly, but later in the future, if you're then going to rip out those fittings, we need to make sure that it's returned to its original state.

Gyms need a different kind of insulation and flooring. Hairdressers need a different type of plumbing to their basins to make sure they're complying with beauty therapy requirements. And the list goes on and on and on. It's always very industry specific.

Over time, we've seen so many industries and so many tenants, when we do due diligence for our clients we have a standard due diligence list plus some that are specific to the tenant, their business, and how they operate the business. We explore outside factors, such as foot traffic, property location, whether it's suitable to many different types of tenants, and possible upside and extensions. We also check rate per square metre and previous sales evidence.

Something that is not often explored is what makes this tenant stay in these premises rather than another premises. It's not just about rent per square metre, but the fit-out, parking, amenities, foot traffic, whether it's in a tenant hub and so on. There are lots of factors that make up that rent per square metre that your tenant pays.

So, don't just look at the rent and say it's unrealistically high. Look at other factors that support the rent and see if they're valid. For example, a medical tenant or a brand name tenant will always pay top dollar. On the surface, you might think that they're paying a really high rent, but if they have A-class fit-out or they're brand name tenants or they're medical tenants, they pay a different rate. Make sure you compare apples with apples when you're going through the due diligence period.

COMPLIANCE DUE DILIGENCE

During due diligence ask your solicitor to seek the compliance documents from the vendor. Believe it or not, the vendor does not have to sell you a compliant property, so it is up to you to check if the property is compliant. The most important one is fire compliance.

If you are unsure, get a specialist fire compliance company to do a report.

Asbestos compliance is stringent across all states, however many vendors are still ignorant of it. This is something we always check as part of our due diligence. Asbestos is not a deal breaker, but you need to know how risky it is. Therefore, getting an asbestos report is a good option if you are unsure. The vendor is meant to order and pay for the report, but sometimes you cannot wait for it so it is best that you get it along with your pest and building report.

Electrical is to do with the meter board, power supply and wiring. When we do an inspection on the property our client is buying we always take a photo of the electric meter to see if it has been upgraded or if it will need to be upgraded soon. Also, depending on the property and the tenant, we need to make sure there is enough power to the property. Trade tenants often need three-phase power, so we need to make sure the premises has that in place.

PROPERTY DUE DILIGENCE

Property due diligence is about the structure of the property. A standard pest and building report can bring up any issues in your commercial property, but I need to caution you here. There is always going to be wear and tear in any commercial property, just like residential, so there is no point in negotiating getting a toilet seat or a tap replaced. In commercial, everything is about functionality. And if the tenant has done the fit-out, then it is their responsibility to get it fixed.

What you are looking for in a pest and building report for commercial is upcoming capital works — things that are going to cost you money within the first 12 months — such as roof and gutter leaks, broken or cracked driveways, pillars and footings that are not secure. Basically, anything that is structural.

ROOF, PLUMBING AND AIR CONDITIONING

When you look at the roof, plumbing and air conditioning, what you should think about is what major spending will you have on the property in the next 12 to 24 months. These are the items I would seek to get the vendor to fix for me, or to give me a reduction in price for. If there are items that need to be replaced or fixed in the next three to five years, then you won't get a discount. Take a little of the positive cash flow each year and put it away so that, in three or five years' time, if you might need to patch up some of the roof or put new air conditioning in for the tenant, you'll have the money to do this.

The biggest expense we see in commercial is the roof, followed by air conditioning. Air conditioning can be very specific to the tenant's needs. I have seen data companies where the air conditioning cannot be down for more than 24 hours. There are also steel manufacturers in open space warehouses with no air conditioning. Then there is air conditioning for funeral parlour and beauty salon tenants, or a whole floor of ducted air conditioning for a national tenant. Each system and the timing varies. If you are unsure, get an air con specialist to check the air conditioning as part of your due diligence.

Roofs may seem scary at first, but know that you don't necessarily have to replace the whole roof. You can reseal a roof or change the roof sheets on certain areas and over time a whole roof can be replaced. It's all about planning ahead and keeping your eye on what's coming up. I cannot stress enough that keeping up with the maintenance of your commercial property is imperative to your long-term commercial property success.

If you are buying a strata property, you don't need to do a pest and building inspection, but you will need to do a strata search (in all states except Victoria). The strata search will show what capital works have been done, and what is upcoming, and if there will be special levies raised. If you are buying strata, you need to check if there is enough in the maintenance/sinking fund to cover any upcoming major capital works, and if not, how they plan to raise enough money for it.

WHEN IS DUE DILIGENCE COMPLETED?

It's hard to know when due diligence is complete, because how long is a piece of string? Each client is different and each of them has different expectations. And it's different for each property. Some may take longer, and others take less time.

You'll know if this property is right for you once you have gone through your due diligence — you should feel either more certain or uncertain about the property. Remember not to sweat the small stuff. If there are red flags, you can always terminate and get your deposit back. Everything is negotiable under due diligence — within reason — so if you really want the deal, don't push too hard. Leave some breathing room for all parties.

NEGOTIATING A DEAL

Due diligence is not about you getting everything you want but coming to an equitable solution so all parties win. When you're in a seller's market as we are now, you cannot afford to negotiate on all the little things. There are big things, such as roof replacements, air conditioning, and structural issues that you can definitely negotiate on. But if there's a hole in a gyprock wall that will cost $500 to patch up, that's not something worth negotiating on. Look at the big picture and how much cash flow the property is going to bring you.

I have had a client complain about a loose toilet seat that only cost a hundred bucks to replace. These are not the things you negotiate on. You negotiate on the main things to secure the deal. For every property you buy moving forward, a handyman or three days on site can probably solve all of those little things. And if that's the case, don't negotiate on those items. Negotiate on the bigger things.

Even if it's a buyer's market, small things are what will annoy the vendor. And if you upset the vendor, they can pull the deal, and you don't want to do that. There's a very fine line between negotiation and ruining a deal because you are nit-picking about it.

You can find out more information about our due diligence process by subscribing to my YouTube channel — Commercial Property Road Show with Helen Tarrant — or on cashedupcommercial .com.au or helentarrant.com.

KEEP YOUR DISTANCE

Sometimes I get clients who really want to be part of the whole process, to get into the negotiations and talk to the agents. They start thinking the agent is their friend because the agent has been so helpful in getting them all the due diligence and information they want on the property, and the agent calls them and talks them through everything twice a week.

Well, guess what!

The agents are invested in the deal, not you. They are not your friend. They work for the vendor. If you side with the agent, it becomes really hard when it comes to the final negotiations. I've had clients miss out on getting roof repairs done and price reductions, all because they bypassed us. They went to the agent and they became 'friends'.

If you engage a buyer's agent, then please let them do their job. They have your best interest at heart, and will fight for you. If you bypass them, you will not get the best result.

TAILOR YOUR NEGOTIATIONS TO THE PROPERTY

If you are buying a set and forget property, you can afford to negotiate harder. You are buying a finished product, and are paying the market price for it. As such, you can negotiate a lot harder on all the items to make sure there are no additional costs coming up in 12 to 24 months.

On the other hand, if you are buying an uplift property where you are going to add value, you have very little room for negotiations. You are taking the property as is. The whole point of it is that you're going to add value to it so it will be worth more, so it's counter-productive to go back and ask for more money off due to it being run down. You'll frustrate everyone and end up losing the deal.

PREPARE FOR SETTLEMENT

Once you have done your due diligence and have your valuation come back on contract price and your loan approved you are ready to go unconditional.

By now you should know your property inside out and soon you will be a commercial property owner.

Once you go unconditional, in two to four weeks you will settle on this property. During that time the bank will send you mortgage documents to sign. They will want you to put the funds into a bank account in preparation for settlement. Next steps are for you to make sure you have the right insurance in place for your property, get a quote for a depreciation report if you want one and then seek out a property manager.

There's lots to do within two to four weeks to get ready for settlement, but if you do nothing else at least make sure you have insurance before you settle and have a property manager in place.

Your solicitor and buyer's agent, if you're using one, will guide you.

ASSESSMENT PROCESS AND DOCUMENT CHECKLIST

There has been a lot of information in this chapter, so here is a checklist of the purchasing process and the documentation needed, to bring it all together. Check out my YouTube channel, Commercial Property Roadshow with Helen Tarrant – there are videos on due diligence and inspections so you can see visually how it is done.

Also for additional due diligence documents check out cashedup-commercial.com.au.

STRATA PROPERTIES — OFFICE SUITES, SHOPFRONTS

The first documents to request are:

- ☐ Information Memorandum (IM). This document gives you an outline of the property, the tenant and the local area.

- ☐ Lease. A detailed document on how long the tenant is there for, how much the rent is and any outgoings that the tenants pay for as well as rent increases and reviews.

Once you have decided the property has the right yield or is the right type of property for you, then you need to ask for the following documents:

- ☐ Annual General Meeting (AGM) minutes
- ☐ Most recent strata minutes

You then read through the minutes to look for:

- ☐ any major repairs that have been done to the property
- ☐ any major repairs that are due
- ☐ schedules for future special levies
- ☐ any pending or current law suits (legal action by the strata or the strata being sued)
- ☐ air conditioning service/replacement (this is the biggest potential cost for large commercial buildings).

Once you are satisfied by the minutes for the strata then you would start the process to put in an offer:

- ☐ speak to your broker about finance before making an offer
- ☐ speak to the sales agent to get a rough guideline on sales price
- ☐ check for land tax for the property and for your personal circumstances
- ☐ decide on the entity you are going to hold the property
- ☐ find out if any rental increases have been applied as per the lease.

FREEHOLD/FREESTANDING BUILDINGS

The first documents to request are:

- ☐ rates notice

- ☐ land tax assessment (if applicable)
- ☐ building insurance (or an estimation as the vendor may not supply them to you unless you buy the property)
- ☐ outgoings:
    - ☐ water
    - ☐ electricity
    - ☐ building repairs and maintenance
    - ☐ any air conditioning maintenance.

Once you are satisfied with these documents then you would start the process to put in an offer:

- ☐ speak to your broker about finance before making an offer
- ☐ speak to the sales agent to get a rough guideline on sales price
- ☐ check for land tax for the property and for your personal circumstances
- ☐ decide on the entity you are going to hold the property
- ☐ find out if any rental increases have been applied as per the lease.

Put an offer in via email and list out any downside you feel the property has and the reason you are making the offer at the price you have chosen. Also put in any conditions you want on the contract. These can be:

- ☐ subject to finance (only applicable in certain states)
- ☐ subject to building and pest (only applicable in certain states)
- ☐ subject to inspection (you viewing the property in person)
- ☐ subject to due diligence (only applicable in certain states).

Once the offer has been submitted:

- ☐ The offer may be accepted, countered or rejected.

- ☐ If the offer is accepted the agent will issue a sales advice and get the contract drawn up.

- ☐ Read through the contract to make sure it has everything you want in it.

- ☐ Take the contract to your solicitor and pay the deposit (which varies from property to property).

- ☐ Perform your due diligence, finance and inspection before the contract goes unconditional.

- ☐ Make sure you get your valuation and building report back before the contract goes unconditional. This will ensure the property stacks up to what it is supposed to be.

- ☐ Make sure your finance is in place before settlement and liaise with your solicitor regarding the process of conveyancing in your state so you are on top of when you need to do what next to complete the process.

- ☐ Wait for settlement and get your solicitor to write to the tenant (if there is one) once the property settles.

Well done — you are now a commercial property owner!

FINAL THOUGHTS

This chapter has been heavy going with lots of information and you may be feeling overwhelmed. If you're starting out my tips are to invest in some education, and subscribe to my YouTube channel—visual learning here is really important. Don't try to understand how to do deals in all the states of Australia. Choose

---

one state you are comfortable with and learn how things work there. Get some information memorandums. Find a couple of properties you like, run the numbers and work it through as if you are buying. Nothing like practice makes perfect here. In fact, this is what we do with our clients: we give them case studies to work through so they can get a clearer picture of what they want and the type of property they want to invest in. This will help you not to have cold feet when you actually do come to buying.

Do check out cashedupcommercial.com.au to get more information.

CHAPTER 11
OTHERS JUST LIKE YOU

I really want you to see that everyday Australians just like you are achieving success via commercial property. We have heaps of client stories and testimonials and they are all unique; here are five stories of different clients from different walks of life that I want to share with you. Hopefully you can relate to some of these stories.

Some of these clients have spoken at my events to present their stories. When you have finished reading this book if you want to reach out to any of them, we are happy to pass on their information to you so you can verify for yourself that this success is achievable.

All the names in this book are real, but I have omitted their surname for privacy reasons.

AN INTERVIEW WITH JOEY

Joey has three kids under five. She works as a fire compliance consultant in her own business, and her partner, Diane, is a dentist with her own practice. When Joey first came to me three years ago, she had 11 residential properties and was highly negatively geared. She had plenty of equity and no way to access it because she was serviceability tapped out. What Joey wanted was to have cash flow so she could support her kids through private school. We worked out she would need around $120 000 positive cash flow to meet that goal.

All Joey's properties were in Sydney so she also had a massive land tax bill each year. We needed to get out of Sydney. Using the money she had in an offset account, we went looking for a regional high-yielding cash flow commercial property.

Figure 11.1 and table 11.1 show the details of the first property we found her in 2019. It was a set and forget and the tenant took up their option to renew in early 2022. (Option negotiations can be a bit of a back and forth, and having a good property manager paid off in this instance.)

Figure 11.1: Joey's Gympie property

Using the cash flow from her first deal she managed to refinance one of her residential properties and pull out another deposit the following year to buy another regional property. This time we needed to find something with a slight uplift.

Table 11.1: Joey's Gympie property

Location	Gympie, QLD
Tenant	Beaurepaires (Goodyear & Dunlop Tyres [Aus] Pty Ltd)
Lease term	5 + 5 + 5 years
Net rent	$82 000
Yield	7.74%
Purchase price	$1 060 000
Current value (2022)	$1 350 000
Interest/mortgage repayment	$37 100 (based on 3.5% interest on the total purchase price)
Positive cash flow after interest	$44 900
Cash on cash return	11.23% (based on a $400 000 deposit)
Return on investment (ROI)	12.74% (7.74% yield plus 5% capital growth)

We found her a property in Bundaberg — see figure 11.2 and table 11.2 (both overleaf). It's a two-storey building with the first floor vacant and the ground floor tenanted by an employment organisation. The employment tenant took up their two-year option in May 2022.

Joey is now on her third property, this one in Townsville. We saw an opportunity for uplift: it was run down, the tenants were on month-to-month leases and half the property was vacant. We made a deal with the vendor who just wanted the headache gone and put the property under contract. The contract was completed by end of May 2022 with settlement by end of June 2022. It took six months to get the property to a level where Joey could finance it. In the space of us working with her and the agent and the vendor over three to four months we managed to get the property 70 per cent tenanted so it could go to finance and valuation.

Figure 11.2: Joey's Bundaberg property

Table 11.2: Joey's Bundaberg property

Location	Bundaberg, QLD
Tenant	Ground floor: Max Employment Solutions First floor: vacant
Lease term	2 + 2 years (for the ground floor tenant)
Net rent	$67 930
Yield	7.27%
Purchase price	$935 000
Current value (2022)	$1 250 000
Interest/mortgage repayment	$32 725 (based on 3.5% interest on the purchase price)
Positive cash flow after interest	$35 205
Cash on cash return	10.8% (based on a $325 000 deposit)
Return on investment (ROI)	12.27% (7.27% yield plus 5% capital growth)

Joey has never visited the property. We have and have sent her videos; she knew she had to put in around $70 000 to $80 000 in capital costs as part of the uplift. The property was secured for $835 000 but after uplift based on the current yield it will be worth minimum $1.1 million. See figure 11.3.

As you can see, the property is not flash at all but the main thing is it has good foundations and potential for multiple tenants and high yield when the uplift is done.

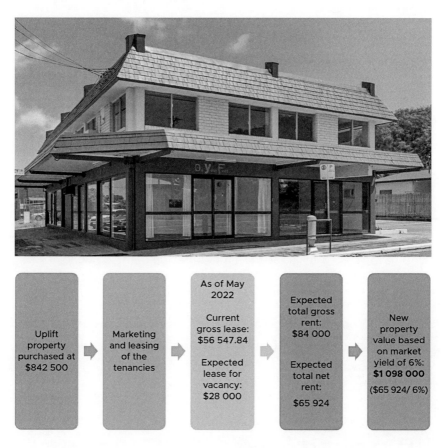

Figure 11.3: Joey's Townsville property

Here is the edited and condensed transcript from an interview with Joey during our last bootcamp.

Helen: So, Joey, how long have you been with us now?

Joey: I think just over two years. I think I joined at the end of 2019.

Helen: Okay. It feels like it's been forever.

Joey: I know. It does, doesn't it? I still remember the days when we used to meet up at Eastwood.

Helen: It's been an interesting journey. So, tell us why you decided to get into commercial in the first place, when you first came on?

Joey: Okay. I remember that I have quite a few residential properties in my portfolio and I get to the stage where the bank just won't lend me money anymore. They just keep telling me I don't have the servicing. So I was thinking, there must be another way to earn money. I cannot just stop. So, for some reason, I was Googling and you came up, and lucky you were in Sydney and you were in Eastwood, which is not far away from me. So I decided to show up to one of those meetups that you have, one of the evenings that you have there. I think, at the time, I met up with someone. The couple that sat next to me, they were onto their second property. They were saying how great their experience was. They purchased their first property the previous year and now they were onto their second one. You just gave me a really good feeling. So that night I think I contacted you. I said, 'Please help me.'

Helen: Tell us about your first deal.

Joey: My first deal was at Gympie. It was a national tenant. We got it for just under $1 million, I think.

Helen: Yes. Beaurepaires. That's part of your retirement plan?

Joey: This is what's going to put my kids' educations through. My kids' education plan, I think. I think at the time I said to you, 'I have a kid and I'm having a second one soon.' Or whatever it is. And I said, 'I need cash flow positive investments, because all my residentials were negative-geared and it was just really bad.' Every month I was actually just pouring money into a bottomless well and I'm not getting any back. This was first cash bought positive property that I had purchased ... It settled on Valentine's day.

Helen: That's a good present.

Joey: My first love.

Helen: Yeah, with love. Definitely. Look, this property we did ... Also, we had, talking about due diligence, I remember at the time, we looked at it, we looked at the bottom of the foundation, because they were storing a lot of tires. There was the insurance issue, because of the tires being flammable. We had to go through all of those little things. Everything is so individual about it. Then we're, of course, going well, the tenants are in the middle of a five-year lease, we gotta go and renegotiate the leases, and we started talking through all the possibilities and things like that. But, since then, the yields definitely have compressed. We're in a different time. But then, you got cash with this one, what did we end up doing as the next deal?

Joey: The next one we got was at Bundaberg. That one was a really, really good buy as well. We have a, not a national tenant, but a government tenant downstairs. They're a recruitment agency. Now, we bought upstairs and downstairs at the same time. It was a strata block. Upstairs, the vendor had it in her super fund. So we literally got a bargain.

Helen: So this is the deal. It is a whole building. We bought it for about $710 000. Upstairs was another $200 000 or so, there was a recruitment agency that had left and they just left so much furniture and everything else there. Potentially, we have to gut the whole place and bring it to a bare shell, because it was just a bit of a rabbit warren. Downstairs, you guys had Max Employment Solutions down there. I know then, unfortunately, when we settled on this, which was towards your late October, then we had the whole COVID situation where office spaces didn't become popular and people didn't want to rent it... But the whole thing is, you never know what kind of tenant you're going to get. We always thought that we were going to get an employment type of tenant there, because it matched. A professional type tenant might need the furniture and everything else, but life didn't turn out to be that way, because we ended up having a yoga tenant.

Joey: Yeah. No, that's really great. As I said, at the time when we got the loan, they were saying to me, 'If you get the bottom, that's the one that's going to keep you going. But if you get the top tenant, that's the cream on top.' So anything on top is just bonus.

Helen: Yeah, absolutely. So we did. We just signed the heads of agreement [which is an agreement by the tenant to enter a lease for the premises] on it. I think, today, I saw the quote coming for the carpet, we'll have a chat to you later about the carpet and helping do the refurbishments for this tenant, on a new five-year lease. So that's good. And for more than what we thought. All along, we were saying to you, 'Look, we probably wouldn't be able to get $30 000. We would probably be aiming for $25 000 and everything.' But we end up getting a tenant for $30 000 a year, which was great.

Joey: Yes. So, it's actually worth the wait.

Helen: Yes, it was definitely worth the wait. Look, this just shows the market does bounce back. And sometimes when you're doing these things, you can't really anticipate. So, what's the plan now with this new property, now that it's got the tenant in there? Are you moving on to the next one or...

Joey: Yes, I am. Definitely. You know that there's another one that is in the pipework. We are just waiting for that.

Helen: I will show you guys a quick snapshot of that one. Look, that one's a bit messy. It's going to take a long time, probably the next couple of months, for us to tidy it up. We've had it under contract for a little while now. But the reason for that is that there was a lot of stuff to be done on the property, and we know that if it goes to valuation at the moment, it just won't value up. The agents know that, so they're helping us do all the things. This is in Townsville, it's an older style property.

It's a solid building, but it just needs some love and care. So, last speaking to the agent last week, they've cleaned up the front section of the restaurant section, because when we were in Townsville we gave them some suggestions about opening the area up. We suggested removing one of the walls, so when people can look in, it's an open space. So they've removed that. They did a really good clean, because there's nothing worse than people coming in for an inspection and not having it clean.

Joey, in terms of how much handholding we've given you through the process...

Joey: Honestly, you're literally still holding my hand at the moment. You know what? I'm so glad I have you guys, because every customer that you have, every one of me, you made it personalised. It's not one-size-fits-all. I feel that you really, really do listen to what I want and you actually go and source the buildings that actually fit my criteria.

When we finish this one, we're going to look for the next one in the next six months.

There's Joey's story! Joey is now earning close to $80 000 in passive income. Once Townsville is finished it will be $100 000. Once we complete Townsville for Joey, we will be sitting down with her for half a day and going over her long-term goals again, looking at what has been achieved in the last three years, next steps for her portfolio and then making the next purchasing decision with her.

TYLER'S STORY

When Tyler bought his first commercial property he was the youngest client we had. He came from a referral: we had helped Tyler's dad, who is a builder, buy an uplift property in Maitland. We found Tyler a set and forget property (figure 11.4 and table 11.3), also in Maitland, so his dad can help him out with some works if needed. Tyler was in his early twenties when he chose to buy his first investment property, choosing commercial instead of residential.

Figure 11.4: Tyler's Maitland property

Table 11.3: Tyler's Maitland property

Location	Maitland, NSW
Tenant	Endeavour Sunnyfield Pty Ltd
Lease term	3 + 3 + 3 years
Net rent	$33 000
Yield	7.76%
Purchase price	$425 000

Current value (2022)	$600 000
Interest/mortgage repayment	$14 870 (based on 3.5% on the full purchase price)
Positive cash flow after interest	$18 125
Cash on cash return	12.94% (based on a $140 000 deposit)
Return on investment (ROI)	12.75% (7.75% yield plus 5% capital growth)

The strategy behind Tyler's property is that he needed to be able to get into his second one sooner rather than later in order to pursue his passion in photography. As such we needed to find a property with cash flow to help with loan repayments and a slight uplift at the back so he can get into this next deal.

I'll let Tyler tell his story here — this is edited and condensed from a bootcamp where he presented.

So this is the property that Helen found me about two years ago, which is 98 High Street in Maitland. So a little bit about the property. So it's about 1250 square meters. The purchase price was about $425 000. We'll get a little bit more into that a bit later. But anyway, the lease at the time was about $33 000 per annum, plus all outgoing, so we were about, I think 7 per cent was the yield on it. However, with the whole yearly increases, I think we're now up to like $36, $37 000.

The length of the lease was a three by three by three, and we were about seven months in. However, we're just about to reach the end of the first three years, and the tenants have given me way in advance notice saying, 'Hey, we want to stick with the option.

We're going to take up the next three years', which is not a surprise with this tenant because they are actually a really great tenant.

Speaking of which, why is this a good property? It is a stable tenant. So they're a disability group where they take care of disabled people, where they come and do activities with them and all of that. They're part of Sunnyfield, which you might see them around here and there as a big corporation. They've got a few places which they're operating from.

But the other big thing on why it's not a surprise that they're taking up the next option is that the tenant has spent money improving the property, and, you know, the moment when the tenant is spending their own money to improve the property, they're not going to be just wanting to pick up shop and just leave and disappear. It's not going to be like the mum and dad operating a fish and chip shop who'd just be like, 'You know what, this isn't our thing anymore.' They've actually invested their own money to improve the property so they're of course planning to be here long term.

So improving the property, so what have they done? There's a shed that they've built, an outdoor area, working on the car park, they've built their own disabled access bathroom. And if any of you who have gone into this before and looked at disabled stuff, you know disabled bathrooms, disabled ramps and all that are ridiculously expensive so it's good that they've been the ones to pay for that.

So the back area was a rainforest to begin with, but they've come in and completely just reshaped that and turned that into a nice garden. I actually haven't seen it since they've actually properly done it up. I should probably go see that some time.

The other thing is it's in Maitland, which is on the outskirts of Newcastle, so it's both close to Sydney and Newcastle, it's not metro like Sydney. Newcastle, as some of you know, Newcastle is getting big and I guess as you can say, gentrification is coming along, that it's spreading out and I guess being two years down the track, I've started seeing some capital gains, which is good. It's always a nice thing to see.

But one of the things that really stood out to begin with was the fact that there were some boundary issues, which we're able to get it at a bit of a discount and fix the boundary issues and make a capital gain straight off the bat. The rear boundary was not properly defined, it was based on a mean high watermark from an old creek, which was a lot of years ago, decades ago. The thing was that it was called a limited lease title, I believe was the terminology, which means the boundaries hadn't been properly defined. The bank didn't want to finance it at the asking price of $550 000 because of that so I came to Helen to solve the boundary issue. Luckily, working with Helen, they know property. They knew that, 'Hey, a limited lease title, worst case scenario we're losing like maybe 30 centimetres off this back boundary.' Which I think it wasn't even that, I think we lost like five centimetres off the back boundary or something crazy like that.

We ended up engaging a surveyor to fix the boundary and register the land to the department of lands. I guess this is the thing: when you see properties with an issue it's always worthwhile instead of just freaking out and running like everyone else is, looking and thinking, 'How much would it actually cost to fix this issue? And how much of a discount can we get off of the property because of the issue?'

Thankfully having Helen being able to do all her negotiating, they were able to bring the price down to $425 000, which we ended up buying it for. It was a pretty steep discount going from $550 000 to $425 000.

Stamp duty and legals, surveyor update to update the boundary, the legals to register the plan. Basically, we're in it for $450 000, which I don't know about you guys, but we paid $451 000 and agents sold it for over $500 000 twice. But the bank wouldn't finance it because of the title. Paying that little bit extra to end up at $450 000, we ended up with a $50 000 capital gain straight off the bat basically after it.

Because we ended up sorting out all the title and that, being conservative with the numbers reaching $500 000 would be a fair thing if I wanted to sell it straight away. But being at 7 per cent yield was like, 'What? Let's hold on to this for a while.' And also knowing that, hey, it's a stable tenant. And knowing that, hey, gentrification's probably coming around the corner eventually.

We paid $451 000, the bank valuation that came back I think was like two months ago or maybe three months ago now. The bank valuation ended up at $600 000. So thinking of it on a financial aspect, we made an initial capital gain of $50 000 and over two years, a further capital gain of $100 000.

So thinking logically I entered this deal with about $150 000. I think I started with a little bit less than that. Basically, I've doubled my money in two years' time, because I ended up with total capital gain of $150 000. So I guess the other question is 'So where now?' The thing is I've started talking with Helen 'Hey, let's get into the next deal.'

There you have it! If you are happy to rent instead of buy a home and invest in commercial you can grow a positive cash flow portfolio. In reality Tyler probably could have bought his next property within 12 months of getting into his first commercial deal, but he was working and happy to let the property sit there and accumulate more equity and refinance it when he is ready to do his next deal. Currently Tyler is earning around $25 000 from his Maitland property per year in positive cash flow and with the equity gains he can easily service another deal.

BRUCE'S JOURNEY

You are the first people to read Bruce's story. He hasn't presented at our events yet; this property is still in the process of being finalised as of writing. I have put more details of Bruce's property in chapter 12.

Bruce is in his mid fifties. He has worked in sales before and had his own business; he's had residential property but lost it all because he couldn't sustain it after business break up with his business partner.

Remember how I talked about how commercial property supports itself so even if something happens to you it can be self sufficient, but residential needs you to support it so if something happens to you then essentially you lose the portfolio too? This is a classic example of this.

Bruce had about \$130 000 saved up and really wanted to get started in commercial.

The fastest way for uplift is always buying a vacant property and re-tenanting. So, we looked at different opportunities and found a property in Toowoomba (see figure 11.5, overleaf). The vendor was an old lady going into a retirement village. She was not very forthcoming and kept changing her mind so it took a while to get this deal through to contract.

Bruce bought it vacant at \$435 000. It was large open space retail with a roller door at the back. We sent one of our team up to see the property and did a virtual tour with Bruce.

While we were there, we worked out the best way to separate the tenancies because it was too large for one tenant. So, we ended up with three tenants. See figure 11.6 (overleaf).

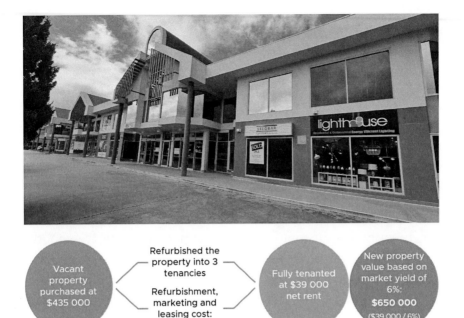

Figure 11.5: Bruce's Toowoomba property

Then we engaged the agent to go and find potential tenants so we could firm up the layout. We got a mobile phone repair shop that didn't need street access or exposure as they are an approved Apple repairer so clients will find them. They wanted the back section so we worked out a layout that would work for them. The property needed new paint plus flooring done and possibly new air con. The tenant agreed to do their own fit-out if Bruce put up a dividing wall, which he did. The agent sourced all the trades plus the quotes for us.

The front tenant took a while to find. They were in the travel business and nervous about going into a premises again. We gave them a rent-free period to incentivise them, and they wanted the front because it was glass-front exposure.

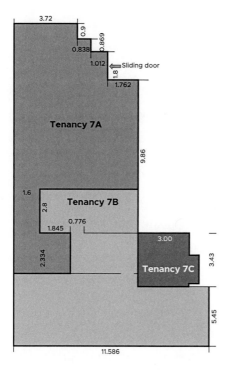

Figure 11.6: floor plan of Bruce's Toowoomba property

Finally there was one little section at the side of the property we thought could work for storage for a business, but the agent ended up finding a single operator architect who wanted to move out of his home office.

While it sounds simple it took four to five months to put together. Including the time under due diligence and finance it took around six to seven months.

The end result is by the end of May 2022 the property was fully tenanted. Bruce will have spent around $30 000 in refurbishment and marketing and agent fees. He got an 80 per cent LVR loan for the property: $110 000 with costs. This was at the max of Bruce's budget and he had to save hard during the purchase process to be able to find enough money to get the refurbishments done.

Now he has a property giving him $39 000 in net rent after outgoings and a uplift in yield (return) of 9.17 per cent based on the purchase price of $425 000. From May onwards with all the tenants in Bruce will have around $27 000 of passive income per year after paying the mortgage plus an uplift in value of the property of $150 000. He literally doubled his money in six months. A lot of work and liaising on our part but also for Bruce; a lot of time to focus on it during evenings and making phone calls to tradespeople during his lunch and break times from work.

The yield in Toowoomba is around 6 per cent so with $39 000 net rent the property is now worth $650 000.

The plan is that Bruce will wait six months, collect the cash flow, then start his refinance: pull out the equity and then go again.

The big picture goal for Bruce is to re-build what he has lost within the next five years, so he needs to be very active doing uplift deals over the next five years so he can build himself a good base.

AN INTERVIEW WITH STEPHEN

Stephen came to us about three years ago. He is a builder, and he was in the middle of completing a massive residential build when he came to me. He has been working on this house project for almost ten years. It is one of the largest and most luxurious houses in Sydney on the waterfront, costing over $50 million. However, because it was coming to an end, Stephen was looking for an option to generate cash flow and he was in the process of selling some of his residential investments for a deposit pool to leverage.

Figure 11.7 and table 11.4 is Stephen's first deal. It was bought in 2019, and the figures are done based on his purchase in 2019. The tenant has since taken up the option for another five years and the value of the property has also gone up.

Figure 11.7: Stephen's Singleton property

Table 11.4: Stephen's Singleton property

Location	Singleton, NSW (bought in 2019)
Tenant	Celnaj Metal Manufactures Pty Ltd
Lease term	5 years since 2016 plus option taken up in 2021
Net rent	$115 775
Yield	9.57%
Purchase price	$1 210 000
Current value	$1 800 000
Interest/mortgage repayment	$42 350 (based on 3.5% interest on the total purchase price)
Positive cash flow after all outgoings and interest	$73 425
Cash on cash return	18.35% (based on $400 000 deposit)
Initial return on investment (ROI)	14.57% (9% yield plus 5% capital growth)

Below is a transcript of our YouTube interview where he explains how he is now earning $72 000 from his first commercial property.

Helen: So Steve, tell us a little bit about yourself and how you got in commercial, or what made you decide to get into commercial?

Steve: All right. Well, I've been looking around at property since 1993, I guess. And decided, like everybody, that residential was the way to go because you buy residential with the aim of getting a capital gain at the end of a few years when you sell it. And the whole concept behind my strategy in the beginning was to buy property, admittedly negatively geared, with the aim that in a certain period of time, it'll be worth a lot more than what I paid for it. Now as much fun as that is, and in time stuff has got capital gains, but on the way, most of the time you're actually taking money out of your pocket to pay for this property. And the challenge with that is there's only so many of those you can buy before it sends you broke.

So I started looking around to try and find a better option. Now I saw Helen's course in October last year, October 18, and watched it — the whole two day thing. And I thought, 'Wow, this sounds like a better way to go.' So I got in touch with Helen's group, and we met by phone a couple of days later and talked about how we can go forward, what sort of properties that she looks at, she invests in. And she introduced me to a property at Singleton, which is inland from Newcastle, New South Wales. It was not an exciting property. It's a warehouse that's got an electrical wholesaler in it. They sell electrical products to builders.

Helen: So you weren't excited about the colour of the building or the tiles or the…

Steve: No, it wasn't like you'd walk into a waterfront mansion and you go, 'Ooh, that's beautiful. Look at the view. Look at the infinity pool.' It was like, 'Oof, that's a nice cash register back there. I have to have myself one of them.'

So we had a look at the property and drove up, and that was a fun-filled three hours on a hot summer afternoon. I really enjoyed the sweating. And ultimately bought it. Now it cost me $1.25 mil. And to make this easier for people to understand why I like it so much, I've got a property in Davenport, Tasmania, it's eight units, and it's worth $1.4 million. Now let's assume we have the same amount of money borrowed on both of them. That's $800 000. The Tasmanian one, after all the expenses, is giving me around about $30 000 a year in my pocket.

Helen: You could really live on that.

Steve: Well, you could live on that. I just don't like camping that much. There's not a lot of air-conditioned tents. So we're talking $1.4 million worth of property, owing $800 000, and at the end of the year it's giving me $30 000. Look at the Singleton one that Helen found for me. It costs $1.25 mil, so we're in $100 000 less by the time you consider legal and stamp duties. Same amount of money borrowed, but the difference is every month it gives $6000. At the end of the year, that's $72 000, less purchase price, same loan. What's that? $42 000 a year more.

Helen: So for some people who are starting on this journey, that $72 000, is that like after all expense are paid?

Steve: That's after everything.

Helen: What about mortgage? What about all the things?

Steve: After all of that, after I paid for everything, council rates, which the tenant pays for, land tax, which the tenant pays a little bit of. After everything, it is $72 000 a year.

Helen: So in your pocket, you can just go on holidays with that.

Steve: Look, I could go on a really good holiday for $72 000. You could buy a small island for $72 000.

Helen: You could. You could. So how did you feel when you first saw that money coming in?

Steve: Oh, it was a life-changer. Because every time, with the Tasmanian one, a lot of money came in as well, but then I had to pay for all these bills. I had to pay council rates at $10 000 a year, and water rates at nearly $10 000 a year, and all this money went back out. And the bizarre thing about the commercial one is most of it didn't go back out. It was like, 'Ooh, hello. That's nice.' So it was a totally different feeling. And it's over double the cash flow that the residential one does.

Now, I'll be honest, when I first thought about going into this, I had the same fears and nervousness that everybody does. It's like, 'Ooh, it's commercial. I haven't done that before. What happens if the tenant leaves?' Hang on. If the tenant leaves, you go and find another one. But you look at this shop and they've spent thousands of dollars on fixtures and fittings and everybody knows where they are. They've got a lease for the next three years. They've been there for, I don't know, 15 years already. So, if you think about it, if you owned a business, why would you want to move? Unless the business goes badly wrong, you wouldn't. All your customers know where you are. You've already spent all the money to set it up. Why would you want to move? So, in some ways a commercial tenant is less likely to move out than a resi one.

Helen: I think that's where most people have the stumbling block is that they see that people have a lease for three years and a three-year option. And they kind of just see what happens in the three years. They think that 'Oh, what if the tenant is just going to pack up and leave?' But, the tenant has spent hundreds of thousands of dollars, and they've got a huge amount of stock. It's impossible for them to sort of just go, 'Okay, well our lease comes up next week. We're just going to pack up and go.'

Steve: And you wouldn't want to. Even everyone who's moved house knows how much brain damage it is to get the lights connected, and the water connected in your name, and get the internet on and deal with Telstra and all that sort of fun stuff. Imagine doing that in a business, right? Then you got to reprint all your stationery. You've got to reprint your business cards. You got to get a different phone number if you go to a different area, so people can't get in contact with you anymore. It's just not the sort of thing that a business would want to do unless they're downsizing.

And once I got into the first one and got comfortable with the fact that these tenants don't want to move because it's going to cost them an absolute bomb, it made perfect sense to go commercial.

Helen: So now you are a commercial property investor?

Steve: Yes.

Helen: You've converted.

Steve: I'm a convert. Praise be the commercial.

Helen: And what tips would you give to newbies? So, people who have never invested in commercial property, thinking of getting into it, what is some advice you can give them?

Steve: Well, the first thing is to get educated first. Go and do Helen's course. She covers every single aspect of the whole purchase, the whole looking at the market. She does everything for you. And you learn everything in two days that you never knew you didn't know. And I know that sounds like a ridiculous statement, but when you first start on this journey, you've got all these questions in the back of your mind and it's like a weird foreign language. But two days in it's like, 'Ooh, hang on. I understand this now.' And then you can go forward with a lot more certainty and start your journey.

So, step one is get educated. Step two is get yourself ready, because you've got to have your company set up, and you've got to have your tax returns and all that sort of fun stuff.

Helen: So, getting structures done?

Steve: Yeah, getting structures done, get set up. And you'll learn how to do all of that at the course. The next thing is to forget everything that you thought you knew about commercial and start to think about some positives rather than all the negatives. If you look at factories or industrial properties or shops that are all around you, and you look at some of them, they've been there for 20 years, 30 years. There's an electrical wholesaler near my house that I've been shopping at for 40 years. It's like, 'Well hang on, if all these businesses have been there for a long period of time, maybe the whole tenant running away in three years isn't a thing.' Think about it based on just looking around yourself and how many places have been there for an awful long time. And they've been paying good rent to someone for an awful long period of time.

There's a lot of people who own commercial property and don't have to work anymore. You know, $72 000 in your hand every year is going to change your life.

Helen: Absolutely.

Steve: It has mine. So, there you go. Thank you, Helen.

Helen: Yeah. Well, thank you. This is what I always say at property seminars, that McDonald's is in the business of real estate, but they're in the business of commercial real estate and not residential. And the Harvey Normans of this world, they didn't make their money through selling franchises. They made money because they owned and built the building that their franchisees are in. That gives them perpetual income.

You've really got to think about some of our big hitters in this market have made their money through a commercial property rather than residential. And maybe residential is at this moment in time not performing as well. And there's another time for it. Maybe right now the next step for some of you out there is commercial property.

Steve: Absolutely.

Stephen has since the first commercial purchase bought four more commercial properties. He has done some uplift deals, sold one and bought another one. All in the space of three years. Stephen's goal is to have $1 million in passive income. So far he's 40 per cent there and the journey to his outcome will be another five years of active investment, doing uplift and set and forget commercial property deals.

DON'S STORY

Don's story is a bit different; most clients prefer to be more secure and stick to metro city investments. Don has built $250 000 in passive income over four properties, all regional, with some in mining towns. It's definitely a case of fortune favouring the bold.

Don found two properties himself and two through our buyer's agency program. Figures 11.8 and 11.9 (overleaf) are the two we found for Don based on his profile.

Gympie (figure 11.8 and table 11.5, overleaf) was his first one. It was a multi-tenanted property that had three tenants on short leases. One of the dentist tenants was going through a transition to a national tenant buyout at the time of the purchase. This property wasn't your typical set and forget like Stephen's Singleton property. This is more of a cash flow–driven property that needs work to tidy it up. This is for someone who is a bit more experienced in commercial property and isn't risk averse. It took a bit of negotiations to get all the tenants on longer leases as set out in table 11.5.

Figure 11.8: Don's Gympie property

Table 11.5: Don's Gympie property

Location	Gympie, QLD
Tenants	Tenant 1: On Location Boutique
	Tenant 2: Jetset Hair Studio
	Tenant 3: Totally Smiles
Lease terms	Tenant 1: 3 + 3 + 3 years
	Tenant 2: 5 + 5 + 5 years
	Tenant 3: 5 + 5 + 5 years
Net rent	$61 840
Yield	8.69%
Purchase price	$712 000
Current property value (2022)	$1 000 000
Interest/mortgage repayment	$24 920
Positive cash flow after interest	$36 920

Cash on cash return	15% (based on a $240 000 deposit)
Return on investment (ROI)	13.69% (8.69% yield plus 5% capital growth)

Don later came back to us to help him find another property and at his request we went to Mackay.

Mackay has only two major economic drivers — mining and tourism — so it is still fairly risky. Both mining and tourism can be volatile so the economy goes up and down. Figure 11.9 and table 11.6 (overleaf) show the multitenanted property we found for Don. It had short leases but very stable tenants so we decided that it was worth buying and then spending time afterwards tidying up the leases to make it more secure. This is more of an uplift property strategy.

He has presented at our bootcamps regarding his journey, so here are snippets of his story as told by him.

Figure 11.9: Don's Mackay property

Table 11.6: Don's Mackay property

Location	Mackay, QLD
Tenants	Unit 1: Pamper Paws Unit 2: Mason Construction Unit 3: Accent on Stone Unit 4: Jeff's Bikes and Bits Units 5 and 6: Thommo Tyres
Lease term	Unit 1: 1 + 1 year Unit 2: 1 + 1 year Unit 3: 2 years Unit 4: 1 + 1 year Unit 5: 3 years
Net rent	$115 430
Yield	9%
Purchase price	$1 282 000
Current value	$1 500 000
Interest/mortgage repayment	$38 460 (based on 3% interest on the total purchase price)
Positive cash flow after interest	$76 970
Cash on cash return	15.39% (based on a $500 000 deposit)
Return on investment (ROI)	14% (9% yield plus 5% capital growth)

My name is Don and my wife and I have a seven-year-old boy. We're based in Sydney and we've got two full-time jobs. Pre- the commercial journey, we had two investment properties. One was negatively geared and one was slightly positive.

As a family, what we were looking for was additional income and looking at, 'How do we replace our income, or how do we get another source to be able to build a foundation and leave a legacy for little Francisco?'

Back in 2017, there was a lot of…I was suffering from shiny object syndrome. There seems to be so much in this property game. You could do property development, you could do rooming, you could do Airbnb, you could do commercial obviously. At that stage, there was a lot of overwhelm because there's so many great strategies. You go to one seminar and you'd be taught one strategy and it'll look interesting so you pursue that. And then the next seminar that you go to talks about something completely different. There was a lot of overwhelm at that stage. And when we sat down with the wife and the little boy, it became, 'What do we want?'

And what we wanted was I guess, what a lot of people want, is a bit of time and freedom and the ability to do what you want when you want. So we investigated commercial property. It was a vehicle in which you can get passive income from day one. And we looked around and we found Helen. When we found Helen, things started to change for us because in terms of…We talk about the A team, you talk about knowledge and experience, Helen is the real deal. When we met Helen, I was actually in the middle of my first commercial deal. I found this commercial deal just in a forum, and someone didn't have the right financing for it. It was a deal in Dalby, Queensland, it was an industrial site.

It was a 12 per cent net yield, it's a big 10 000 square metre block. And the fundamentals stacked up for this one, which is you had an anchor tenant there. They do essentially these massive water tanks in Queensland and they've got offices across Queensland, New South Wales, Victoria and Western Australia. And this national anchor tenant had been there from 2003, really solid in terms of fundamentals. Their revenue's about 20 million, the operational costs are pretty fixed. The deal just stacked up because the nature of the business was solid. And so, I took this on, it had three tenants in there, so the national tenant plus two other tenants. And what I liked about this deal was the upside potential. Because of the land space and where it was, potentially you could build some storage sheds for additional income but you could also do a telecom tower as well for Vodafone or Optus.

I purchased this property at $855 000, the rent income per year is roughly $124 000. I do have an agent to manage the property because it's three tenants and it was my first property. The insurance cover was $3000, which is for fire and loss of interruption. If there is a fire, they'll pay for a year's loss of income, which is good. And I've got the loan for this one, eventually got the deal and the positive cash flow income is just about $65 900 per year, which is great.

Okay, the next one. At the time I was doing that first deal, we met with Helen and I knew within 15 minutes...that Helen's values were consistent with ours. And she really knew her stuff, which was really, really great. I thought, 'Let's get into a deal.'

This one is in regional Gympie, Queensland, it's a multi-tenanted property that was four different tenants. Well, four lots within the premises, one of them was vacant. We bought this at about 8 per cent net yield but since then, it took me about three months to get the vacant tenant...I got a council that signed up for that vacant tenant and they just pushed up the yield to 10 per cent. The anchor tenant here was a dentist. The dentist actually has a five year lease, five on five with options and increases of 4 per cent. But the dentist decided not to continue business around December. They stopped, they let go of staff but they're still paying the rent.

And that's something that really surprises me commercially, is that you've got a dentist in this premises who's signed up for a five year lease with increases, and who have decided to move. And the reason for that is they're part of a big multinational...Let's say franchise, and they've just decided to move from Gympie but they're still paying the rent, so that even though there's no revenue, they're still paying the rent for that. Things are good for that. We've also got three other tenants on that, which was strong leases with increases each year, as well. That's been a really, really good find. And I thank Helen for this one.

One of the amazing things about commercial versus residential is that the outgoings are paid by the actual tenant. And it's not uncommon that you see that in a lot of the leases, which is fantastic, is what you don't get in resi. In terms of purchase price, the purchase price for this...I think the purchase price started around $750 000 to $760 000, around that price point. And this is one of the values that you get from Helen. She's amazing in a lot of things but one of them is negotiation and actually pitching the right price. And she negotiated this one even further down. We signed the contracts. We paid I think, 2 per cent deposit and within the due diligence, we found a few gaps and issues within the property. Some of the lights falling down and that's things that work in your favour. As you negotiate within that due diligence, you can actually get a further price reduction and Helen managed to knock off a few thousand on that, which is great.

There was an agency fee, we were happy to pay for that. The rent on that was $72 000 and interest on that was $30 000. The total annual cash flow on this property is $41 700. And look, you were thinking COVID, a lot of businesses would suffer some issues. And a lot of them did. In this case, the hairdresser tenant asked for a bit of rent relief for 50 per cent for a few months just to get them by. They're on the JobKeeper or JobSeeker, one of the two. They've been able to maintain that level of business. The fashion shop, the other shop there, they've asked for just one month of 25 per cent rent relief but they've been able to maintain that level of cadence and revenue. They're still paying their rent on that. It's a really good outcome on this one, so that's pretty cool. And when you start getting that income, it becomes real because then that income builds up for your deposit for your next deal.

And the next deal, deal number three happened probably about three months after the one in Gympie. This one fell in my lap. I was talking to an agent about six months prior to this, about another deal in a regional town. It was actually a bank at the time. And at the time, I thought, 'Banks are a bit risky. They're pulling out from regionals because their strategy is to reduce operational costs across the country.'

I thought that was a little bit risky but he gave me a few calls and he's got… This one was interesting, given the fundamentals on this one. This deal went from $1.7 million to $1.4 million in a span of three months, so chipping away. And when you get to talk to the agent and build that relationship, what we found was that this tenant is quite an established tenant across the country. And really, when you're buying commercial, you're really looking at the business model and you look at the strength of that business model. Obviously, there's a layer with COVID but you look at the strength of that business model and is it able to sustain its growth? And this company established in '88 roughly, but it's grown through acquisition. Its model is about buying these smaller companies, its competition, and actually growing through acquisition and just being a dominant monopoly or dominant player within the company. The vendor who sold the property, he was competing within this regional centre.

And the big company just said, 'Look, well, there's an offer you can't refuse.'

And obviously he's taking it. The big companies bought this business and then the vendor just wanted to offload the property, and that's why we were able to negotiate that reduction in price. That national company does big major machinery for mining and agriculture. In this place, it's Emerald, which they've got two major mines, and it's also got the biggest agriculture in the southern hemisphere for all citrus fruit. And yeah, it's just acreage. They've got demands not only for the mining companies but agriculture too. A 13 per cent net yield, which is very attractive.

The rent on this was $187 000 per annum, the interest cost on this one was $39 000. The annual cash flow on this is $148 000 per year, which is great. And obviously, as I mentioned, the outgoings are paid by the tenant. And working with Helen... obviously, she's a great mentor

Next Helen found this wonderful property, again in Queensland. We're very Queensland centric but that's okay. We're actually diversifying now with syndicate deals and stuff. Anyway, the deal on this one, fundamentals again, quite strong. When we spoke to Helen, obviously the fundamental's been about the business. This business is about training, they do training workshops for project managers, administration work, forklift drivers, et cetera. They've got 11 offices around Australia. It's a family business, headquarters in Brisbane. Obviously the net yield on this one and the lease was quite strong, but there's three titles on it. There's uplift potential on this one. For example, if the tenants decide to downsize, then you can lease out the second one or you've got an opportunity to do some construction, which could be some storage sheds, get rid of the parking lot. And so the options are there. The lease is quite strong. It's three on three with two, three options with CPI increases.

What have I learned from this experience? Being really clear on your goals is very important. Is it passive income or is it another source of income or replacing your income? What is it? Be very specific on that. Be very specific on your risk profile as well. You hear risk reward, the higher the yield, the higher the risk as well. I'm a project manager by trade. My bread and butter is analysing risk. And once you understand the risk, you can understand the action or the remediation that you need to do.

There you have it. A very different profile. Most of Don's properties are in high-risk mining towns. This may be too high risk for some but depending on your life experience you may be totally comfortable with it.

FINAL THOUGHTS

It's important to remember when looking at these case studies that everyone's journey is different. Your first purchase may look nothing like any of these case studies. That is okay, because your pathway is unique and individual. The most important thing to remember is that in commercial property investment you need a team of people to support and guide you. Unikorn Commercial Property can give you this but if you want to do it alone, find a good mortgage broker who can tell you if the deal is going to work with the bank or not; find a good solicitor you can refer to for due diligence and advice; and an accountant who is going to be able to help you with the right entities for asset protection and tax minimisation. Look at commercial property from a strategy point of view; in order to create a pathway to financial freedom, you have to design it, create it and implement it.

Every commercial property deal is a live deal so don't expect to get your ducks in a row before you make an offer or start the buying process. You will need to work through all the bits and pieces, like putting together a 1000-piece puzzle, to get to the complete picture. Then you can decide if you are happy with it or not.

Bear in mind markets change over time and, depending on which market you are in, it will vary how much you can negotiate. Ultimately buy something that lets you sleep at night.

I have so many stories from the last decade of helping clients getting in the right commercial property. At the end of the day for me the motivation for helping others is that I *love* commercial property, but I LOVE changing people's lives more. For me this is a calling. Every day my reward is seeing how the cash flow has changed everyone's life. I always say personal development is great motivation, but nothing beats positive cash flow in your bank account at the end of the month. Seeing that money and knowing you can spend it whichever way you like frees your mind, it empowers you to do more. It gives you choices in life and it starts to give you some breathing space so you can start chasing your passion and living the live you deserve.

CHAPTER 12
UPLIFT PROJECTS

Uplift projects are not for the faint-hearted. They need constant attention and work until you can let them operate on their own. In this chapter, I am going to cover the different types of uplifts available in commercial — from the easiest to the hardest. Just remember if you have not done an uplift deal before, please seek professional advice before you do one. You should probably do a set and forget commercial property deal before doing an uplift commercial deal, if you do not come from a previous developer background.

An uplift in commercial property is creating and manufacturing equity — changing the value of the property. In order to do that, you need to understand thoroughly how capital growth and cash flow works in commercial (covered in chapters 5 and 6 in more detail). Once you have a thorough understanding, you can apply it to an uplift project.

TENANT INCENTIVES

If you want to do an uplift project, you need to understand tenant incentives. There are many different ways to incentivise your tenant, but here are the main three.

RENT-FREE PERIOD

This is the most common and widely used tenant incentive. The metrics are that it should be one month per year of the lease term. So, three months rent free for a three-year lease. Usually, for a one-year lease there is none, and for a two-year lease, there's one month. Potentially, there are up to six months rent free for a five-year lease if you have a high-end tenant that is going to do a lot of the fit-out of your property.

FIT-OUT CONTRIBUTION

This is very common if you are a developer and the property is a bare shell. Then you would offer to give your tenant either a basic fit-out to a warm shell, which is air conditioning, flooring and potential ceiling, lights and plumbing and electrical points for their fit-out purposes.

If you are a landlord, this usually applies when you are about to put in a new tenant, and they cannot operate their business until they have a new fit-out. This is especially so if it's a change of use for the property, such as going from a hairdresser to a dentist or to a restaurant. Fitting it out could easily cost a tenant $100 000, if not more. A medical fit-out is $400 000 at a minimum for a two- to three-room practice. If you have a government tenant in your property, they will need it to be disability compliant. This could mean changes to your toilet and a disability ramp. This could be at your cost, which is where the contribution comes in, as it would be cheaper to give the tenant the contribution in cash form than to organise the works.

NO OUTGOINGS FOR A SET PERIOD

If your tenant is just starting and setting up their business, they may appreciate if they don't need to pay outgoings on the property for, say, 12 months or so. This may mean they are saving around 30 per cent of their rental costs and it will be a leg up to getting started. Either way, it's up to negotiations, depending on the length of the lease. If the tenant is entering a new premises, the strata and some of the outgoings may not be set yet, so therefore it may also not be applicable.

***

For any tenant incentive, it's about working with the tenant to help them get started or to relocate to your premises. The cost of relocation is high for any tenant, which is why commercial tenants don't tend to move around much. The fit-out and relocation cost is a sunk cost, so for you as a landlord, making it easier for your tenant to get started will help you out in the ultimate sale price of the property. Make sure you are equitable to all parties.

UPLIFT 101 — TENANT AND SELL

The simplest uplift to do is buying a vacant property and putting in a new tenant. You can be in and out of it within six to nine months, and on a sub-million-dollar purchase you can pick up an easy $100 000.

For example, recently we put one of my clients into a deal in Pinkenba, which is about 5 kilometres outside the Brisbane airport. It's a huge development area for industrial tilt slab properties, and lots of industries there need access to logistics hubs and to the airport. It was new stock that the developer had completed but hadn't sold. The market yield for warehouses in the area was 6 per cent in mid 2021 and it was trending downwards. At the beginning of 2022, it was at 5.75 per cent. This was the perfect market for an uplift.

The warehouse was bought for $852 500, which was the lowest price for the vendor. He just wanted to move it on. We bought and settled on it towards the end of 2021. The property was vacant. In the beginning of 2022, the same type of warehouse in the complex sold for $900 000, so we were already gaining — even as a vacant property. We started looking for a tenant. It took three months to find a tenant and get a new lease with some rental incentives. We stuck to our rent of $63 500 and gave a slightly longer rent-free period to get it. The agent tried to talk us out of it because they had tenants that would offer $55 000 or $57 000 per year for the rent with no incentives. We didn't accept because it would have eroded our ultimate sale price.

When you do a tenant and uplift, you always need to look at the type of tenant, the rent, and the ultimate sale price. You need to make sure you put in the right tenant so you have the right sale price in the end.

In the case of Pinkenba, we wanted a trade tenant because we knew that they would be a long-term secure tenant for our incoming purchaser. After much back and forth, we ended up with a four-year lease to a trade tenant. In the beginning, they didn't want to pay the outgoings, but we ended up giving them a longer rent-free period to cover off the first year's outgoings and they signed the lease.

Soon we'll start marketing the property for sale. We'll try to sell it off market to save marketing fees and some agency costs. The turnaround time is about six months from settling and getting a tenant in and being ready for sale.

The end result should be between the following ranges:

$63 500 / 5.75 per cent = $1 104 300

$63 500 / 5.5 per cent = $1 154 500

See a quick snapshot of the profit in table 12.1 and a photo of the property in figure 12.1 (overleaf).

Table 12.1: potential profit on Pinkenba

Purchase price	$852 500
Deposit (%)	30%
	($255 750)
Loan amount (%)	70%
	($596 750)
Stamp duty estimate	$31 388
Building/strata report	$550
Solicitor/legal costs	$2000
Valuation	$3300
Interest on loan	$35 805
Interest rate	6%
Marketing, legal (5% of purchase price)	$42 625
Outgoings per year	$7000
Total money in over 12 months (including purchase costs and all refurb)	$378 418
Net rent (waived for first year as incentive)	$63 500
Yield (rent / purchase price)	7.45%
Sale price at 5.5% yield (approx.)	$1 150 000
Profit after all costs (if sold after 12 months)	$174 832
Minus sales commission (2.2%)	$23 000
Net profit before tax	$151 830
ROI	40.15%

Figure 12.1: the property in Pinkenba

PARTIALLY TENANTED

Partially tenanted properties are properties that have a holding income, so you are not totally out of pocket. The most likely scenario is that there are three to four tenants in the property, but the property has the potential to have six to seven tenants at full occupancy; the three to four tenants are on short leases (12 months or less), their rents are low, and the property is unloved.

The main characteristic to look for here is if the location is central, to attract future tenants. The property doesn't have to be in metro. In fact, you'll find a better uplift in regional for this type of property. Here is a list of things we like to tick off for these types of properties:

- **key location**: close to other commercial tenants and hubs

- **parking**: has parking for staff and future tenants

- **access**: access to key roads and motorways

- **versatility**: ability to host different types of tenants in the future

- **unloved/run down**: needs cosmetic uplift

- **structural issues**: has some but not major, e.g. some roof sheets to be replaced and gutters, but not the whole roof

- **exposure**: exposure to drive past or walk past traffic

- **layout**: the property layout can easily be modified without huge costs

- **low rent**: the current tenants are paying low rent that can be increased

- **zoning**: the correct zoning to allow different types of tenants

- **refurbishment**: ability to strip the property back to a bare shell and fit-out for a new tenant

- **holding income**: the property is able to pay its outgoings and some of the mortgage while you do the uplift on it. Normally a 3 to 4 per cent yield with the potential to increase that yield by an additional 2 to 4 per cent when completed.

The property does not have to be freestanding. You can do it on a large strata property too.

Here is an example of a partially tenanted property. Joey, whose story is in chapter 11, bought a property with a tenant downstairs. The yield was at 7 per cent when she bought it, and the property was in Bundaberg. Just as she was about to re-tenant, COVID hit, so it took two years to tenant rather than one year (which is more normal). The tenant downstairs was Max Employment Solutions, and they were on a two-year lease with options. Upstairs used to have an HR training tenant who moved out and left all their furniture. The upstairs property hadn't been tenanted for over two years when we found it for Joey. The issue was that the upstairs layout was very messy, and there was furniture everywhere.

Ultimately, it took making it an open plan property, plus a coat of paint to tidy it up and replacing the air conditioning, to get a yoga studio upstairs. The tenants were happy to forgo six months rent free on a five-year lease if we did new floor coverings, which we did. This added an additional $22 000 to the property income, but that was straight into the pocket, because previously when we bought the property, it already had a holding income (which means that the property already has a tenant even though they may not be paying substantial rent or on a long-term lease; this is your upside, to fix up the tenancies and increase the rent). What's more, it brought the yield of the property up to over 9 per cent. The lease was signed in March 2022. Here are the details of Joey's Bundaberg property (a picture of it can be found on page 186, figure 11.2):

- floor area: 236 square metres
- 16 private parking bays with eight allocated for each tenancy
- purchase price: $935 000
- settled December 2020
- net rent: $67 930
- downstairs tenant: Max Employment Solution with two plus two years rent
- upside potential:
  - tenant upstairs to increase yield
  - collapse existing strata to save outgoings to achieve higher yield
  - revaluation to pull out equity for next deal.

The new income upstairs was $25 000 and that made the new rent $92 930. At the current market yield of 7.5 per cent in Bundaberg for this type of property and tenant, it is now worth $1 239 000. If you refinanced the property now you could pull out almost all of the deposit you put into this deal.

If it weren't for COVID, this could have been turned around within 12 to 18 months, but it's taken over two years to do. That's the risk you take doing an uplift property, because you don't know how long it will take to re-tenant. Ultimately it's always about risks versus reward. The greater the risk, the higher the reward.

DIVIDING UP SPACES

One of the first uplifts I did as a commercial property investor was to take a big space and turn it into more functional smaller spaces. If you think about it, it's like what Westfield do. They take a large building, divide it up into smaller premises, and rent them out at higher prices.

You can replicate this strategy on a smaller scale, either as a new build, a freestanding building or a strata unit.

Below is exactly what Bruce, whose story is told in chapter 11, did. He bought a property vacant as one premises, and then new gyprock walls were built internally to create three tenancies. He put in new flooring and paint, plus new air conditioning in one of the tenancies. All up, he spent around $20 000 to $25 000 on capital works. With leasing fees on top, we'll end up with a net rental income of around $40 000. At a 6 per cent yield, the new value of this property is around $660 000. Even after entry and exit costs there will still be around $150 000 in uplift in this property.

This was Bruce's first property. He only had a limited deposit to get started, and needed a way to get into a second deal. So, this was a high-risk leap for him, but it paid off in the end. All of it was done remotely, while Bruce was in Sydney. The agent in Toowoomba handled it all.

Here are the details of Bruce's Toowoomba property:

- purchase price: $435 000 bought vacant
- floor area: 193 square metres
- upside potential:
  - three doors so you can create three different tenancies
  - well-located complex with little vacancies
  - large regional town
  - plenty of parking
  - ease of access for tenants being ground floor
  - shared amenities in the building already.

This was the simple strategy of getting a bigger property and dividing it into smaller, more versatile tenancies to cater for changing tenant demands.

FINAL THOUGHTS

When it comes to uplift properties, choose your battles. Some properties are diamonds in the rough, or ugly ducklings. Others are just no go, because you are inheriting too many issues. You want fixable issues, not properties with massive structural issues that cost you both time and money for very little return. Having an eye to spot the right commercial uplift deal takes time and practice, which is why you need to do a set and forget property before you attempt an uplift property.

When you do a commercial uplift, remember you need to make the premises versatile and functional, rather than beautiful. So many investors coming from the residential space want to spend extra to make the property beautiful. But that's not going to add value to the rent or the property. Find out what your tenant specifically wants and give it to them in the fit-out. That will add value to the property.

Uplift properties are not for the faint-hearted, so make sure you engage professional advice when you get started. Do your numbers and build in contingencies.

Many investors make the mistake of wanting to do an uplift property but planning to use set and forget strategies. But if you want to create uplift then your tenants will be on short leases paying under-market rent; the property will need some TLC and there may be capital works to be done on it in the first 12 months of you owning it. Your tenants may be complaining about how nothing has been done on the property for years (or decades) when you do the inspection. This is all part and parcel of doing an uplift project. You are essentially buying someone's headache, and the upside is to take the bull by the horns and turn the property around within 12 months so you can make a gain in both cash flow and value.

Think of it this way: a set and forget property is like paying a premium to buy a fully-grown tree that already bears fruit. An uplift project is the seedling that may be struggling and desperately needs water and soil to grow. You spend time nurturing it to grow so that ultimately you can sell it to an investor who wants the fully grown fruit-bearing tree.

The upside of having an uplift property is that, even if the rent is not to the same level as you expect it, you can always hold the property a little longer to get the sale price you want. And the positive cash flow coming from the tenant in the first year while you hold it will compensate for any loss or additional expense you incurred.

If this is the pathway you want, I encourage you to go and check out my YouTube videos and reach out to me, so I can show you some case studies and feasibilities to give you a better understanding of how the deal works.

I also encourage you not to do your first uplift project alone. Seek mentorship and guidance because there are a lot of pitfalls and choosing the wrong property could mean you don't get the uplift you want in terms of final sale price, or hidden problems that will cost you thousands of dollars.

CHAPTER 13
SAILING OFF INTO THE SUNSET

Everyone asks me the question: When do I sell my commercial property? Some of my clients invest for the long term, and are looking to build generational wealth. For them they NEVER want to sell. But for at least 50 per cent of us, at some point we think of selling.

The question is always: When is a good time to sell? Real estate agents will tell you to sell when the market has gone up, because you can cash in. However, if you have nothing similar or with better returns, there's no point in selling and then putting your money in the bank for less than 1 per cent return.

The smart move with selling is to repurpose those funds. In commercial, you would sell a few smaller starter properties to get into a larger commercial property. Here are some of the reasons why and when you should sell.

WHEN YOU HAVE MADE A BAD BUY

In a rising market, if you've made a mistake with any of your property purchases, it's worth getting the property tidied up and then selling it. This is the best chance for you to make your money back — and then some. Typically, in commercial, a bad purchase means the tenant has not been performing, and that there are capital works to be done on the property. In a rising market, it makes sense for you to incentivise the tenant to go on a longer lease, and to also complete the capital works so you can sell the property at its best price point.

Sometimes you may only make a little. Or you may make a small loss. But consider the opportunity cost of holding on to the property. It would be better leverage for your money if you bought elsewhere once you got rid of a non-performing asset. Also, in a rising market with a lower interest rate, you'll find that a lot of owner-occupiers want their own premises. So you may find that it's easier to sell your property to an owner-occupier. Make sure you explore your options, and speak to at least three commercial real estate agents before making a decision. Also, visit your property to see what needs to be done. You may need to repurpose the property to get it sold.

I recently did that for a client of mine. She had a property that the tenant vacated during COVID and we couldn't get it re-tenanted due to parking issues. The property was located in Toowoomba, and I went to have a look at it. There was a main entrance and a side entrance. I discovered that if the stairs from the main entrance were removed, and the side entrance had a disability ramp, then there would be three parking spots and disability access. This opened up the potential to lease that property out to a NDIS (National Disability Insurance Scheme) tenant or allied health tenant, or perhaps even a dentist. Once you have one of those tenants, you can sell the property at a much higher price point, because there is now security in the tenant. Currently, with Toowoomba achieving yields around 6 per cent and compressing, it's a good time to do the refurbishment and then sell the property.

TO BUY A LARGER COMMERCIAL PROPERTY

If, when you first started in commercial, you could only afford a $300 000 or $500 000 property, and over a few years you bought a few of those smaller starter properties, it's time to consolidate them and sell them. This means you can combine the gains plus any deposit you have now, and your original deposits from all the other properties, to buy a larger property.

If you can go from a $1 million property to a $2 million property, the value changes dramatically. And it's the same if you can go from $2 million to $4 million. You get a much bigger footprint, and the growth of your property and income can double by going up a tier.

The ultimate goal is that you want to be able to access properties that have a higher price point. The lower the price point, the lower the return, because competition is so high for properties with a lower price point. With the recent upsurge in residential prices, and baby boomers heading into retirement, there's a lot of cash about — and everyone is looking for a cash flow return. So, if you are buying below the $1 million category, the competition is fierce. If you can look at a higher purchase price, you eliminate the competition and have more options — plus higher returns. And higher returns mean more cash in your pocket, and potentially higher capital growth in the future.

When you come to sell, everyone focuses on the capital gains tax, and how much they need to pay. Instead, look at the big picture, and the cost of lost opportunity. I suggest you put capital gains tax on a payment plan and pay some interest on it. With any property, you need time in the market. The more you wait, the less the returns. This is evident if you look around at what has happened in the last two years in both residential and commercial. Let the new cash flow from your larger commercial property pay down your capital gains tax debt.

TO BUY INTO A DEVELOPMENT

One of the questions that always gets asked during the purchase process is: Why is the vendor selling? A lot of vendors sell to get into a development to maximise their returns. The dream we chase is passive income. But ultimately when you retire, you may want a balance of active income as well as passive income. One of the best ways to achieve an active income, while you have the choice of working or not through your commercial property, is to do developments. If you have set and forget properties, you'll find that at some point, in order to get to the next level, you'll need to do an uplift or a development deal. Sometimes this will require you to sell one of your commercial properties to have more cash to buy a larger commercial property. Ultimately, it's all about bulking up your commercial property portfolio, and keep growing it.

FOR RETIREMENT AND DIVERSIFICATION

When you first start out in your commercial property journey, you accelerate and leverage as much as you can to get to the next level. Then you spend some time tweaking and maintaining your property. And ultimately, you consolidate by selling some of your properties so you can lower your debt and de-risk your portfolio.

YOU'VE HAD THE MAXIMUM VALUE FROM YOUR PROPERTY

You should sell if you've had the maximum value out of that property — if you bought it well, experienced exponential growth in the property to the point where you can no longer extract the value out of it. It's about your ability to extract value, not someone else. Not an incoming purchaser. Nor what will happen in the future in the market. We're not speculating about that.

Suppose you bought a $500 000 commercial property a couple of years ago when you started out. We'll assume that you bought it well, at a 7 per cent yield. Now the market has changed and everything else is yielding 5.5 or 6 per cent in that area. In the two years you've had the property, its value has increased — most likely somewhere around 20 to 30 per cent given the market movement in recent years. Going forward, is it likely to do double-digit growth for the next two to four years? If it isn't, what are you missing out on? This is the interesting question, because people don't look at lost opportunities. What they look at doing is holding on to their property in case the market grows again. But that's the wrong way to think about it.

You should consider if you've extracted the maximum value out of your property for yourself, and for your portfolio. Because if you have, then it's absolutely the right time to sell and upgrade to the next one. The reason for that is if you hold on to it, after strong growth, it's likely a diminishing return. So the next year you may have 5 per cent more, and the following year, 10 per cent more. But you're never going to have another spurt of 20 to 30 per cent.

For example, one of our clients bought a warehouse for $900 000 on the Sunshine Coast at 7 per cent yield, right before COVID hit. The Sunshine Coast has boomed through COVID over the last two years. That property today, with the rental growth he's had over that time, is now worth $1.2 million. This is about 35 per cent growth in that property now.

Going forward, is it going to go from $1.2 to $1.5 or $1.6 million in the next two or three years? The answer is most likely not. And if it's most likely not going to happen, then you should definitely sell that property today, this year, while the market is still attaining that growth. Sell. Take the proceeds and the deposit you put in (around 20 to 30 per cent) — something like $300 000. Now you have almost $600 000 to do a bigger deal. If you leverage that $600 000, you could buy something like a $1.8 to $2 million property. So you're not only going from $900 000 to potentially buying a $1.5 million property. You've gone from $900 000 to potentially buying a $2 million property.

Now, the return on a $2 million property is two-fold. Firstly, it takes you out of the pack of mum-and-dad investors, who can invest $500 000 or below $1 million. Secondly, it puts you into a more serious investment category. It gives you more choices in a market where it's heated for properties below $1 million. It allows you to potentially buy properties that give you a better footprint, a better return and a better choice of tenants, or versatility in the future. Or you look at back-buying into metro where we may be seeing more accelerated growth, after the growth is finished in more regional areas. So you should absolutely sell that first property.

TO BUY YOUR ULTIMATE RESIDENTIAL HOME TO RETIRE IN

Commercial property is a cash flow game — just like residential is all about capital growth. The Australian dream was that you buy a residential home and pay that off. Then the trends changed to investing and renting where you want to live. Recently, I have more and more young clients who are buying their first commercial property rather than residential. They're investing in cash flow to help them build up a more robust deposit so they can buy where they want to live. Also, having the cash flow from the commercial property helps them to rent somewhere better. If you invest in an uplift commercial deal, then add value through changing tenants, doing a refurbishment or creating a more lettable area, then you should have a timeline when you should sell the property. You could either get into a larger commercial property deal or to use the profits from the sale to buy your dream home.

Normally, it would be wise to hold an uplift property for up to a year to get some cash flow to recover your outlay in capital works, or your tenant incentive, and allow the market to mature before selling it.

As a rule of thumb, an uplift in commercial should give you 20 to 30 per cent gross profit. So if you invested in a $1 million property you should get $200 000 to $300 000 out of it, depending on what you need to do. That profit, along with the deposit you put in, could be enough for you to sell out and buy a residential home.

The timeline for an uplift in commercial is typically longer than residential, so allow for a minimum of 12 months.

FOR SUCCESSION PLANNING

The biggest reason we see vendors selling in commercial is for succession planning. It is not uncommon to see a sale and lease-back, because the vendor is the father and his kids are taking over the business. He's selling the freehold property so he can retire. Sometimes there is a partnership restructure for a law firm or an accountancy, and they need to sell the freehold. This is all very common in the commercial space.

When it comes to you being an investor and deciding if it's time to sell, you need to consider what is going to continuously produce income, and what is the most de-risked asset you have. That does not mean you keep all your metro properties. It means that you look at your portfolio and sell the property that is likely to have higher risks in the future. This could be because it is too remote or in a regional area, or if it could take too long to re-tenant. Look to keep the more set and forget properties, and the ones in key locations, regardless of whether they are in metro or regional. Sell off properties that may cost you more to hold over the next five to ten years.

WHEN YOU SELL

When you do sell, make sure you seek advice from your accountant regarding the correct timing in the financial year. And make sure you read your loan terms, so you know if there is a penalty for exiting your loan early.

Set aside money for capital gains tax. Also, look at effective ways to distribute funds to your children, or into your self-managed super fund, to gain the maximum benefit.

Make a logical choice when it comes to selling and not an emotional one. It's about having a hassle-free retirement rather than keeping the property because you are speculating, or are emotionally attached to it.

Further, make sure you prepare for the sale of your property by getting the leases ready, and completing any capital works. It can take three to six months to prepare a property for sale. This is to tidy up the leases, and make sure the tenant is happy and informed. Many vendors don't tell their tenant that they're selling. Personally, I think this is poor form, as your tenant is one of your biggest assets in commercial, and you need to take them into consideration. Make sure you fix any issues with the tenant, otherwise you will run into roadblocks when there is a valuer going through or a buyer inspection.

Finally, speak to three agents and look at their sales record before you decide who to go with. Selling off market is a good idea if you want a discreet sale and if you want to save marketing costs. Weigh up your options before moving forward on the sale, and work out your numbers and baseline, but be realistic on where the market is. A well-priced commercial property should sell within two to four weeks once on the market, or presented off market. A badly positioned one could take months to sell, or not sell at all.

FINAL THOUGHTS

The reason why you should sell your commercial property is unique to each situation, and is up to what you plan to do in the future with the proceeds of the sale. For me, the question is: Have you extracted the maximum value out of your commercial property for your journey? What that means is, has the commercial property you bought served its purpose?

If you're into buying and adding value, then selling, you shouldn't hold on to the property. You should just sell at the end of the project. If you bought a starter commercial property and now you have some more deposit and you can buy a property with a larger footprint, then you should. If you have bought in an area that has boomed, then I suggest that you sell in that area because you have had exponential growth. It's best to cash out and then buy into a different area that hasn't boomed or has gone through a low, so you can capitalise on the new area's future potential.

If you have retired, then you should continuously work on your portfolio. Keep your finger on the pulse of what is happening. When an area has boomed, you should sell and potentially buy a larger property, or two smaller ones to de-risk your portfolio. Think of your commercial property portfolio like a bonsai. Giving it continuous attention will make it grow faster.

CONCLUSION: IF THEY CAN DO IT, SO CAN YOU ...

In 2016, I set out on this journey to teach everyday Australians how to invest into commercial property because there was no-one in the market teaching people about it. By now, I've given you a lot of tips on how to structure the journey of your commercial property investment. There is the foundation of cash flow. You need growth, so that you can tap into the equity and you can continue to borrow. Balancing cash flow and growth is paramount for continued growth in your property journey, regardless of whether you invest in residential or commercial property.

Further, once you start to have some time off and start to work a little bit less, or you're looking for ways to increase the acceleration of your property portfolio, you'll need to do uplift deals, where you are creating equity. That's no easy feat. But with the right mentorship and learning to do it right the first time around, and finding similar metrics to those discussed in chapter 12, you'll be able to rinse and repeat that. Ultimately you'll be able to make a chunk of cash of

$100 000 to $150 000 on the side while you're working, which will continue to grow your property portfolio.

So right now, what do you do? You've heard other people's stories. If they can do it, so can you.

There are many ways and pathways to enter the commercial property space.

When you get started, it's important to belong to a community to see that other people just like you are out there starting the commercial property journey, buying $500 000 properties. Yes, those properties are hard to find in this current market. Yes, yields are compressing. Yes, it is a seller's market and yes, you have to move fast. And we are going to experience more boom in the commercial property space in the next three to five years than we've seen in the past decade. But there is no reason why you can't get into commercial property.

Everyone asks, 'When is a great time to get started in the commercial property buying journey? Should we wait for the market? Should we sit out for 12 months? Should we wait for interest rates to rise?' The thing is, it's demand and supply. There's going to be more demand for commercial property in the next three to five years than there's going to be supply. So regardless of whether interest rates go up, regardless of the yield and the returns dropping, when compared to residential, it's still likely going to have more returns, because there's more cash flow on the front end and you can have growth at the same time.

Plus, more baby boomers are retiring than ever, especially during COVID, and through early retirement, and they're taking their money out of residential and putting it into commercial, or they're cashing out of their businesses or principal homes and buying commercial property, because they need cash flow for their retirement lifestyle.

The competition is fierce out there for commercial property. This is why you must refer to this book and understand the fundamentals and the foundations of commercial property. You must engage a professional to help you and mentor you through the process — even if it is just for the first deal — so you can achieve the financial freedom and the financial returns that you want through investing in commercial property the right way.

The metrics that we look for in commercial property when we're investing are general across your whole portfolio, not only on an individual property basis. The goal is a whole portfolio of a 10 per cent cash on cash basis, which means that you're getting a 10 per cent return on your direct cash deposit, not including growth. And if those are the metrics you work on, all you do is work backwards from your goal to calculate how much deposit you are going to need to be able to finance the lifestyle you want in retirement.

So, if you want $100 000 in passive income, you need $1 million in deposit. Whether you have that million dollars today, in equity or cash or in your super, or you will get to that million dollars through doing an uplift deal, or through savings, or through selling a residential property or refinancing your principal place of residence over the next few years, that's your personal journey.

This is why I encourage you to reach out to us through cashedupcommercial.com.au or to HelenTarrant.com to have a personalised strategy session so you can get a blueprint of your journey through commercial property.

I would encourage you to start with an open mind and forget everything you know about residential. Don't let your own preconceptions ruin a deal or block you from learning what you need to do to achieve success. In commercial always think win–win, rather than fighting over the last dollar. Look at the big picture. Only by doing and actively seeking out the answers can you overcome analysis paralysis.

There is nothing holding you back. All you have to do is apply yourself, know the process, engage a professional, understand your journey from step one to the end, and not quit until you get there. Even if there is a pandemic, even if there is a global financial crisis, even though we might have crazy inflation or high interest rates. All it will do is delay your journey. But it's better to start and end up with maybe 50 or 70 per cent of your positive cash flow goal than none at all.

Which is why I cannot implore you enough to get started now. While the best time to buy commercial property was ten years ago, the next best time is now, today, tomorrow, next week, because you cannot make up for lost yields, lost rent, and lost opportunity.

Invest in education because commercial property is a vocation. Take your retirement seriously. And then take flight on your journey and invest in your future.

NOW IT'S YOUR TURN!

Before I go, I want to give you a few more tips on commercial property.

The commercial property space is fierce and is full of professional investors and institutional investors (such as Charters Hall), syndications that are buying up large shopping centres. You might feel like you're a small fish in a large pond. You might feel lost by the current that is pulling commercial property. You might feel like it's out of control for you. It's important for you to feel grounded, so start with the following action steps.

INVEST IN EDUCATION

Subscribe to my YouTube channel and podcasts.

ENROL IN MY FOUNDATION COMMERCIAL PROPERTY INVESTMENT COURSE

Join and participate in our community. You will start learning and be continuously educated on the changing world of commercial property. Soon we will have physical meet ups back again, so you'll have some likeminded people to talk to and be able to attend the boot camps. You can find out more at cashedupcommercial.com.au.

BOOK IN A STRATEGY SESSION

It's your personalised strategy session, where we're going to overlay the strategies detailed in this book, plus your personal information and where you want to be. Your long-term goals, where you are now, and where you want to be. We'll take into account the things you want to do between now and retirement and your big picture goals. We'll then provide you with a blueprint of what you need to do to achieve this with commercial property. Maybe along the way you'll need to do some residential as well, so we'll add that to the mix.

This is an overall strategy, not just on commercial property, but looking at whether you should be diversifying your portfolio. Whether you should be doing residential first then commercial or commercial then residential. Or maybe you should invest in alternative investment vehicles, such as syndication or funds.

START YOUR COMMERCIAL PROPERTY SEARCH

Start by looking on realcommercial.com for commercial real estate to get an idea of the kind of commercial property that you'd like.

Request some information memorandums from the agents, read through them, get an understanding of what they are and ask questions. Even if you don't know, start asking some questions. Start getting your head around different commercial property markets around Australia and try to conceptualise investing in commercial property — what it will be like for you to buy that particular type of property and get that cash flow!

WORK ON REAL CASE STUDIES

Once you've completed your blueprint, you will be provided with some case studies. Go through these case studies and provide feedback to our coaches. Our coaches will run through them with you, why they're applicable to you, why they are the right properties for you or not, and build out a particular criterion for your first deal.

ENGAGE US IN YOUR COMMERCIAL PROPERTY JOURNEY

Engage us as your buyer's agent or decide to go out on your own. If you decide to go out on your own, then make a list of the criteria you need and start hunting down your first commercial property. You will most likely need to go through 50 properties, 50 IMs, and 50 leases before you get a clear understanding of your first commercial property and what that looks like. Run your numbers and start making offers.

MEET YOUR TEAM

If you do engage us as your buyer's agent, we will surround you with a team. We will take you hand-in-hand from the beginning to settlement and beyond. And you'll always be part of our community where you can troubleshoot in the future. We do the due diligence, the inspections, and mentor you through the whole process till settlement and beyond. You can find out more on the Cashed Up website, cashedupcommercial.com.au.

REFER TO THIS BOOK IN THE FUTURE WHEN YOU ARE CONFUSED ABOUT CERTAIN THINGS

Email us and post on our Facebook group when you want to find out more information about the commercial property that you are buying. Don't be scared to ask questions. Engage professionals. Speak to your lawyers. Really understand the conveyancing process, and know your lease inside out.

YOUR TENANTS ARE YOUR PARTNERS IN CRIME

Make sure that you take care of them. Make sure you speak to them after you settle. Make sure you get to understand their business, so that you can help work with them hand-in-hand to achieve a better outcome for their business and they can stay long-term as your tenants.

HIRE A PROPERTY MANAGER

While you are growing your portfolio, don't get bogged down in the management of your commercial property. Get it professionally managed, so you can focus on the bigger picture. Vet your property managers to see if they have managed your type of asset, if they can negotiate with tenants during hard times and if they can help you with leasing should you need to.

ALWAYS CONTINUE TO ASSESS YOUR OUTCOMES

Are you getting closer to your financial freedom goals, or further away from them? The first three months after buying your commercial property is going to be hectic, and you may still need to tidy up outstanding items. After that, you'll see the forest from the trees, and look to when you can do it again.

YOU ARE READY TO INVEST IN COMMERCIAL PROPERTY NOW

I know it sounds scary, but your time is now! You will learn more as you buy your first commercial property. Putting the education into play is the best and scariest experience of your life. Buying commercial is like a roller coaster as all the deals are live deals. There is a thrill in it and once you start getting the cash flow you will be addicted.

You will NEVER make back lost yield, cash flow and opportunity, so seize the day, soldier forth, and take flight!

RESOURCES

Below you will find a list of resources where you can join, link up and subscribe to continue your education.

WEBSITES

cashedupcommercial.com.au

helentarrant.com

unikorn.com.au

SOCIAL MEDIA LINKS

FACEBOOK

Helen Tarrant
facebook.com/helentarrantcommercialproperty/

Commercial Property Cash Flow
facebook.com/CommercialPropertyCashflow/

Unikorn Commercial Property
facebook.com/UnikornCP/

High Yield Commercial
facebook.com/highyieldcommercial/

Successful Commercial Property Investors
facebook.com/groups/967892983660683

Commercial Cashflow Mentoring Program
facebook.com/groups/1254434834588232

Wealth Club
facebook.com/groups/3769201653202588

YOUTUBE CHANNEL

Commercial Property Roadshow with Helen Tarrant
youtube.com/c/CommercialPropertyRoadshowWithHelenTarrant

LINKEDIN

Helen Tarrant
linkedin.com/in/helentarrant/

PODCAST

Commercial Property Investor Show

Available on Apple iTunes, Google Podcast, Spotify,
Amazon Music, or wherever you listen to Podcasts

EDUCATION LANDING PAGE

COMMERCIAL PROPERTY INTENSIVE

commercialpropertyschool.com

INDEX

acceleration 28–29

acquirable asset rule 149

action to take now 245–249

agents, keeping your distance
from 175–176

air conditioning, due
diligence on 173

apartment in Crows Nest
(Sydney), author's
parents buy 9

Armidale (NSW), buying
properties in 12–13

asbestos compliance 172

assessment process 177–180

asset protection, options
for 119–120

author
—at university 10–11
—childhood in Australia
4–7
—early years in Beijing 1–4
—journey in property 16–18
—parents in Australia 5–7
—work lessons as young
person 8–10

bad buys, selling after
making 231–232

baker as tenant,
questions for 168

Bare Trust Custodian 141

beauty salon
—author's 10–11
—finances of 13

Beijing, author's early
years in 1–4

Belgian Gardens (Qld), property
for over $2 million 154

big picture goals,
creating 57–58

booster loans for vacant
properties 128

boundary issues in
Maitland (NSW) 195

Bruce's property in Toowoomba
(Qld) 197–200, 227
buffer, saving a 146–147
Bundaberg (Qld), Joey's
property in 185, 186,
189–190, 225–226
Bundoora (Melbourne),
professional office
space in 79–81
buying journey in
SMSF 145–146
buying through an
entity 117–120

capital gains, problem with
44
capital growth 43–46
capitalisation rate (cap rate)
75
cash on cash return
73–74, 243
cash flow
—calculating 77–78
—case studies 79–84
—commercial 40–41, 43
—importance of 11–13
—need for 68
—residential 37–40
—residential vs commercial
42
—starting with 58–60
cash flow and growth,
balancing 21–22, 25–27

cash flow property
—buying 25–27
—in Chermside (Qld) 69–70,
73–74, 77
—examples 69–70
cash flow vs growth 70–71
cashing out of SMSF
properties 155–156
Chermside (Qld) cash flow
property 69–70, 73–74, 77
child therapy centre, Robina
(Qld) 78–79
China, author's early years in 1–4
commercial loans 123–124
commercial properties
—author's first 14–16
—buying 24–25
—cash flow from 40–43
—cash flow and
growth in 94–100
—importance of
tenants to 48–50
—preparing to buy 121
—pros and cons of 105–108
commercial property journeys 56
commercial property
valuation 100–101
company, buying through
a 118, 120
competition for commercial
property 243
compliance due diligence 171–177
consolidation 30

contract and process
—New South Wales
164–165
—other states 165–166
—Queensland 161–162
—Victoria 162–164
Crows Nest (Sydney),
author's parents first
apartment buy in 9

Dalby (Qld), Don's property
in 211–212
Davenport (Tas), Stephen's
property in 203–204
de-risking a portfolio 32–34
deals, negotiating after due
diligence 174–176
dentist tenants, needs of 170
developments, selling to
buy into 234
discretionary trusts, buying
through 118, 120
Docklands (Vic), property for
over $2 million 154
document checklist 177–180
Don
—interview with 211–216
—property in Dalby
(Qld) 211–212
—property in Gympie
(Qld) 207–209
—property in Mackay
(Qld) 209–210

—property in Queensland 215
—third property 214–215
double stamp duty 120
due diligence
—different aspects of 166–174
—doing in different
states 160–166

80% LVR low doc loans 126–127
electrical compliance 172
emotion in buying 55–56
encroachment, dealing with 167
end-of-lease time, valuation
at 101–102
entities
—buying through 117–120
—setting up 120

finances
—for restaurant 15–16
—restructuring 122–123
financing a purchase 121–124
fire compliance 171–172
fit-out contribution as tenant
incentive 220
fitness gym, Gold Coast (Qld)
82, 83, 84
freehold properties, documents
to request and offer
process 178–180
freestanding buildings,
documents to request
and offer process 178–180

freestanding property, Belgian
   Gardens (Qld) 154
full doc loans 127

generational wealth,
   creating 28–30
Gold Coast (Qld) fitness gym
   82, 83, 84, 154
Gordonvale (Qld), property
   under $600 000 152
growth, looking for 60–62
growth and cash flow
   —balancing 21–22, 25–27
   —vs repaying loans 147–149
growth properties
   —buying 25–27
   —characteristics 87–90
growth vs cash flow 70–71
gym tenants, needs of 171
Gympie (Qld)
   —Joey's property in
      184, 188–189
   —Don's property in
      207–209, 212–214

hairdresser tenants, needs of 171
Hermit Park (Qld) cash flow
   property 69–70, 73–74, 77

industrial property, pros and
   cons of 108–109
investment portfolio
   example 26–217
investment types,
   comparing 73–76

Japanese restaurant (Sydney)
   —buying 14–16, 30
   —cash flow and
      growth in 94–100
Joey
   —Bundaberg (Qld)
      property 225–226
   —interview with 188–191
   —property searches
      for 183–187

Koolewong (NSW), author's
   property in 11–12

land tax 118
larger property, selling to
   buy 233–234
lease, reading 159–160
lease doc loans 124–125
loan approval in SMSF
   143–145
loan rates, with entities 119
loans
   —repaying vs growth and
      cash flow 147–149
   —types of 124–130
low doc loans 126–127
LVR (Loan to Valuation
   Ratio), effect on loan
   amount 142–143

Mackay (Qld), Don's property
   in 209–210
maintenance 29

maintenance of property 50–522

Maitland (NSW), Tyler's
        property in 192–196

market capital gain 88–90

market rent review 101–102

maximum value from
        property, selling after
        having 235–236

medical professionals, 100%
        loans for 129–130

metropolitan vs regional
        70–72

mixed tenancies, pros and cons
        of 113–114

Mount Street (Sydney) property
    —buying 14–16, 30
    —cash flow and
        growth in 94–100

negotiations, tailoring to the
        property 176

New South Wales, contract and
        process in 164–165

no doc loans 128

no outgoings for set period as
        tenant incentive
        220–221

North Albury (NSW), retail
        space in 82, 83

North Sydney property
    —buying 14–16, 30
    —cash flow and
        growth in 94–100

now, action to take 245–249

offers, making 160–166

office space, Bundoora
        (Melbourne) 79, 81

office suites, documents
        to request and offer
        process 177–178

office tenant, questions for 170

offices, pros and cons of 105–108

100% loans for medical
        professionals 129–130

$1 million plus, properties
        for 152–154

over $2 million properties 154

partially tenanted properties
        for uplift 223–226

partially vacant property 63–64

Pinkenba (Brisbane), tenant
        and sell property 221–223

plumbing, due diligence on
        173

portfolio
    —balancing for cash flow and
        growth 25–27
    —self-sustaining 64–65

portfolio control, with
        commercial
        property 46–48

professional office space
    —beauty salon
    —Bundoora
        (Melbourne) 79, 81

property, type to buy in
        SMSF 149–154

property due diligence 172–174
property maintenance 50–52
property manager, using 48
property price ranges in SMSF
    purchases 151–154
property value, combining rent
    and market value 92–94

Queensland, contract and
    process in 161–162

rainy days, saving for 84
re-purposing properties 232
real estate agent and hearing
    specialist cash flow
    property 69–70, 73–74, 77
regional vs metropolitan 70–72
rent-free period as tenant
    incentive 220
rental growth, effect on capital
    growth 91–92
repaying loans vs growth and
    cash flow 147–149
resi-commercial
    properties 104–105
residential investment
    properties, buying 22–24
residential property, cash flow
    from 12, 37–40
restaurant property
    —buying 14–16, 30
    —finances for 15–16
restaurant tenant,
    questions for 169

retail properties, pros and cons
    of 110–112
retail space, North Albury
    (NSW) 82, 83
retirement residence, selling to
    buy 236–237
Ringwood (Melbourne)
    office property, capital
    growth in 33
risk, minimising 32–34
risk vs security 50, 71–72
Robina (Qld) child
    therapy centre, cash
    flow for 78–79
ROI (Return On Investment)
    —calculations 74–75
    —commercial vs
      residential 36–37
roofs, due diligence on 173

saving a buffer 146–147
security in SMSF purchase 151
security vs risk 71–72
self-sustaining portfolios
    64–65
selling
    —after having had maximum
      value 235–236
    —for succession
      planning 237–238
    —things to do before 238–239
    —to buy into a
      development 234

—to buy larger
   property 233–234
—to buy retirement
   residence 236–237
selling SMSF
   properties 155–156
service offices, Walkerville
   (SA) 79–80
settlement, preparing
   for 176–177
settlement process in
   SMSF 143–145
shopfront properties
   —documents to request and
      offer process 177–178
   —pros and cons of 110–112
Singleton (NSW), Stephen's
   property in 200–207
$600 000, properties
   under 151–152
Slacks Creek (Qld), property
   under $600 000 151–152
SMSF (Self-Managed
   Super Fund)
   —borrowing in 142–143
   —buying journey in 145–146
   —buying within 139–145
   —for commercial
      property 136–137
   —loan approval and
      settlement in 143–145
   —loans 129
   —performance of 135–136

—property prices in 151–154
—property types to buy
   in 149–154
—reasons for 133–135
—workings of 137–139
SMSF (Self-Managed Super
   Fund) properties, cashing
   out of 155–156
South Australia, buying in 166
spaces, dividing up 226–227
specialist assets, lease doc
   loans for 126
starting, best time for 242
Stephen
   —interview with 202–207
   —property in Singleton
      (NSW) 200–201
strata offices, pros and cons
   of 105–108
strata properties
   —Docklands (Vic) 154
   —documents to request and
      offer process 177–178
   —due diligence on
      173–174
   —Surfers Paradise 61–62
succession planning, selling
   for 237–238
Sunshine Coast (Qld)
   warehouse property
   —benefits of selling
      235–236
   —client's 31–32

Superannuation Industry (Supervision) Act (1993), acquirable asset rule in 149

Surfers Paradise (Qld) strata property 61–62

Sydney
—buying residential investment properties in 22–24
—Mount Street property 94–100

Sydney northern beaches property, gain from 33

tax minimisation 118–119

tenancies, separating 197–199

tenant due diligence 168–171

tenant incentives, for uplift projects 219–221

tenant and sell uplift 221–223

tenant vs no tenant 48–50

tenanted commercial properties, buying 24–25

tenants
—needs of different 170–171
—questions for 168–170

Thai restaurant, Chermside (Qld) cash flow property 69–70, 73–74, 77

Toowoomba (Qld), Bruce's property in 197–200, 227

Torrington (Qld) property, for $1 million 152–153

Townsville (Qld), property for Joey 185, 187, 191

Townsville (Qld) commercial property, capital gain example 33

trade tenant, questions for 169–170

tweaks 29

$2 million, properties over 154

Tyler, property in Maitland (NSW) 192–196

under $600 000 properties 151–152

Unikorn Commercial Property, genesis of 16–18

uplift properties
—tenant incentives for 219–221
—warnings about 228–229

vacant properties, booster loans for 128

valuation, at end-of-lease time 101–102

value in SMSF purchase 150–151

value vs yield 89–90

Victoria, contract and process in 162–164

WALE (Weighted Average Lease
Expiry) 76
Walkerville (SA)
—$1 million property
in 152–154
—service offices in 79, 80
Warana (Qld) warehouse
property, client's
31–32
warehousing, pros and cons
of 108–109

Warriewood (Sydney) property,
capital growth in 33
work lessons as young person,
author's 8–10

yield
—definition 76
—vs risk 72
—vs value 89–90
yield compression 89–90
yield values 59–60